London

An Illustrated History

Catherine Mulgan

Edward Arnold

© Catherine Mulgan 1979

First published 1979
by Edward Arnold (Publishers) Ltd
41 Bedford Square, London WC1B 3DQ

British Library Cataloguing in Publication Data

Mulgan, Catherine
    London, an illustrated history.
    1. London — History — Pictorial works
    2. London — Description — Views
    942.1'2'00222   DA677

ISBN 0-7131-0299-3

Set in Plantin 110 and 194 and printed in Great Britain by
Unwin Brothers Limited, The Gresham Press, Old Woking, Surrey.

Contents

Map of London today.

Introduction

If you go into the City of London today, at first you may think that old London has disappeared altogether. It seems as if the City consists only of modern streets and office blocks.

Yet a great deal is still there if you know where to look for it. The easiest places to find are the buildings and pieces of wall above ground level: the Tower of London, parts of the Roman city wall, many old churches and a few private houses.

Far more lies hidden below ground. Workmen digging foundations for new buildings in the City often find objects that are many centuries old. This is because our ancestors threw their rubbish out into the back yard or the street; moreover, when they wanted to build a new house or a church, they pulled down the old one and built on top of the rubble and the rubbish heaps. This continued so long that the remains of Roman London now lie up to fifteen feet below our present street level.

Another survival of old London is the street names. Even when the buildings have vanished completely, a name often gives a clue to where they used to stand. If you look at the map of the City of London today (on the previous page), you will be able to work out the outline shape of the Roman city. Find seven streets with names ending in '–gate'. Imagine a line linking them all, and you have an idea where the Roman wall lay. Like all city walls, London's had a ditch just outside it. Look for a road name ending in '–ditch', and not far to the left of it there is a road actually called London Wall.

Look next for two names ending in '–hill'. These mark the position of the two gravel hills on which the first London was built. Many street names in the City contain the word 'friar' or 'church'. Today you only see rows of offices, but once there were friars living by Blackfriars Bridge, and a parish church in Gracechurch Street.

Try to go into the City on foot, best of all on a Sunday when the streets are nearly empty, and look for yourself.

Fountain Court, Cooper's Row (just to the north of Tower Hill). Part of the Roman wall round the City, with a modern office block looking down on it.

I
Roman London

Two thousand years ago the site of London was almost empty. Only the two gravel hills were there on the north bank of the Thames. More than a thousand years earlier still, there had been a small settlement on the western hill. Possibly there were some huts left at the top of the hill, and a few fishermen's cabins down by the river bank.

There was certainly no bridge, no docks and no town. It is hard to imagine the site of London with only grass and bushes where the tall buildings now stand.

At that time the Thames was much wider than it is now. Several small rivers ran into it, as indeed they still do. But today they are hidden in pipes underground, and only the street names remind us where they are. Fleet Street crosses the river Fleet, and Walbrook goes over the Wal Brook.

Above and below the site of the City, there were marshes on both sides of the river. Only at one point was there firm ground on the two opposite banks. On the south, a narrow strip of sand came right up to the water's edge (where Borough High Street now runs). On the north, the gravel slopes of Cornhill and Ludgate Hill came down to the river bank. You can still see these slopes, especially when there is not much traffic about. You climb up from Blackfriars Bridge to Ludgate Circus and on up to St Paul's; and you go uphill from London Bridge to the Bank of England and the Mansion House.

London had everything a town needed: firm ground on which to build houses, water to drink, forests to provide wood. The river Thames could take boats down to the sea, or up into the heart of the country. Above all, at this particular point there was a fine site for a bridge.

But the few Britons living in the area two

thousand years ago did not need a bridge. Nor did they have the skill to build one. It was the Romans who saw the advantage of bridging the Thames here, and so started London on its career as a great city.

The first Romans came with Julius Caesar in 55 BC. They made short visits both that summer and the next, but did not stay long enough to build anything. Caesar described the river Thames in the book he wrote about his campaigns. His soldiers rode across it with the water reaching up to their necks, but no one knows exactly where this happened.

Caesar always meant to come back and conquer Britain. But he was too busy with affairs in Rome itself. For the next hundred years the only Romans to visit Britain were traders.

When the Romans finally decided to conquer Britain, in 43 AD, they knew a good deal about the lie of the land. Claudius, the Roman Emperor, collected a large army and ordered them to sail across the Channel to Richborough. Next, they were to aim north for Colchester, where the most powerful British chief had his fortress. To reach Colchester, the Romans had to cross two rivers—the Medway and the Thames.

The Britons had no hope against the highly trained, well-armed Romans under their general, Aulus Plautius. They were defeated beside the river Medway, and messengers went hurrying to fetch Claudius, who had remained in Rome. The journey each way took several weeks; meanwhile the Roman soldiers had little to do. It is likely that they built a bridge over the river Thames during this time. Perhaps it was just a line of boats lashed together. Or they may have built a proper wooden bridge, since some of the soldiers were expert engineers. Aulus Plautius and his officers had the skill to spot the best site, where

Roman Britain, showing the route of Aulus Plautius' army.

there was firm ground on opposite sides of the river. (See the map on p. 19.)

Every London Bridge built since then, including the latest (completed in 1974), has been sited near the spot the Romans chose.

When Claudius arrived, all he had to do was to cross the Thames and ride in triumph into Colchester. With most of their leaders dead, the Britons saw that further fighting was useless.

The Roman army was divided into three for the next stage of the conquest. Each of these groups won control of a big wedge of country, setting up forts as they went along. By the end of this campaign the Romans had conquered most of southern Britain.

Soon fresh troops arrived from Rome to help control the newly-won lands. Ship after ship arrived, loaded not only with soldiers, but also with the food and equipment which they would use. At first the ships docked at Richborough. Everything had to be carried north overland, then across the Thames. Very quickly the commanders saw that London was a much more convenient unloading point. So docks were built along the river bank on either side of the bridge. Now the ships could sail across from the continent and go straight up the Thames. Warehouses were built behind the docks, and camps for the soldiers on their way north and west. Next came markets and workshops, and homes for the men who worked in them. Built in a hurry, all these were made of wood.

All this time the road-makers were at work. Wherever the Roman soldiers went they made roads. It was so much quicker to march along a straight, smooth road than through a trackless forest. The first Roman road went from Richborough to London. Others soon followed, stretching out into the newly-won lands like a great spider's web. London was the central point where all the roads met. It was the most convenient place from which to send out men and goods in all directions. Much later, the planners of railways and motorways made it their focal point as well.

People in Rome began to hear more about the new province of Britain and its fast growing towns. The Roman historian, Tacitus, wrote that London was 'crowded with traders, and a great centre of commerce'. This was in 60 AD, only seventeen years after the Romans' arrival.

Boudicca's Revolt

All of central and southern Britain was now under Roman control. Caractacus, the last British chief to go on fighting, had been hunted down and beaten in the Welsh mountains. Everything seemed to be peaceful when the new governor, Suetonius Paulinus, arrived from Rome to take over.

He decided it would be safe to leave only a few soldiers to keep order in the south-east. The main body of the army would come with him to north Wales to attack the island of Anglesey. Here the strange Druid religion had its headquarters. Suetonius knew that the Druid leaders were sending spies into the rest of Britain to encourage people to disobey Roman rule. There would never be real peace till Anglesey was conquered and the Druids were destroyed.

The attack on Anglesey was almost complete when a messenger from Colchester rode in exhausted to tell Suetonius that the Britons were in revolt. Boudicca, Queen of the Iceni tribe, had roused her tribesmen in Norfolk with reports of Roman insults and high taxes. With the bulk of the Roman soldiers far away in Wales, she gathered an army of Britons and seized the chance to attack Colchester.

The few Roman soldiers left on guard were helpless to stop the attack. Colchester was set on fire and all the Romans who lived there were killed or taken prisoner. At last the Britons had a chance to take revenge on the foreigners who had seized their homeland.

Encouraged by this success, Boudicca decided to try to drive the Romans right out of Britain. London, the central storehouse, would have to be destroyed next.

By now the Roman Commander, Suetonius Paulinus, had come back from Wales, riding on ahead of his main army at great speed. He reached London ahead of Boudicca and her men. At once he realized there was no chance of defending it with so few troops. There was one faint hope; he had sent a message to Gloucester

Statue of Queen Boudicca by Westminster Bridge. The sculptor has invented the spikes sticking out from the chariot wheels.

to ask the general there to send help. But these soldiers did not come. Very regretfully, Suetonius Paulinus gave the order to abandon London.

Many people did not get away in time. When the hordes of Britons swooped on the city, anyone found in the streets was rounded up and killed. Boudicca wanted to destroy every Roman building as well as every Roman citizen. Since all the houses were made of wood, it was easy to set the whole place ablaze. Soon all London was burnt to the ground.

Nearly two thousand years later, men digging foundations in the Cornhill area still come across a layer of dark red ash. It lies about fifteen feet (five metres) below our present street level. That is all that is left of the first Roman London.

Boudicca next burnt Verulamium, but just after that the main Roman army arrived back from Wales. At last Suetonius Paulinus had enough soldiers to attack and Boudicca and her Britons had little chance against them. So the rebels were beaten at last, and Boudicca took poison rather than become a prisoner.

Rebuilding London

Now it was safe for the survivors to come back to the piles of ash and charred wood which had once been their homes. London was rebuilt as quickly as possible, but this time much more stone was used. The main buildings were made completely of stone and tile. Houses and shops often had stone foundations and wooden walls.

Town planning was straightforward to the Romans. They just had one basic master plan which could be adapted to suit every site. Whether the town was in Britain or Turkey, Spain or North Africa, you could always tell it was Roman. Everywhere there was the same grid plan with a market place in the centre.

Some modern cities have a similar lay-out, notably New York. It might be simpler to find places in London today if the Roman plan had survived. Unfortunately, it was all built over in a much more random way in the middle ages.

While the rebuilding went on, the government in Rome decided to make London the capital of Britain instead of Colchester. Already London was the meeting point of all the main roads. It was much more central than Colchester, and it was growing more rapidly than any other town.

Now it was the capital, London also became the home of the Roman Governor. He was the most powerful man in the country; the Emperor in Rome appointed him to run the Province of Britain. While modern government needs tens of thousands of civil servants and enormous office buildings, this was not true in Roman and medieval times. The officials who worked for the governor had their rooms in one part of his palace.

As with many other places in Roman London, only careful detective work has shown where this building stood. The first clue turned up over a century ago when workmen were building Cannon Street Station. They noticed pieces of mosaic buried in the earth they were digging, and the bases of very thick walls. Unfortunately no one thought of recording or protecting them. A hundred years later, foundations were dug for a new office block just to the east of the station. Again the workmen found the remains of unusually thick walls. They seemed to be in the shape of several large halls, and also many small rooms all about the same size. Some of the tiles

The Governor's Palace. An artist's idea of the Palace, with its entrance porch at an angle to the main building. The drawing is based on archaeologists' findings on the site.

One of the tiles found on the site of the Governor's Palace. 'P.P. BR. LON' stamped on the tile stands for 'Publicani of London in the Province of Britain'. The publicani were the government tax-collectors.

found on the site were stamped 'P.P. BR. LON'; this was the trade mark of the Romans' state brick and tile factory.

The archaeologists (who had been called in this time) were almost certain that this had been an important government building. But who exactly had used it? The plans were compared with those of government buildings in other parts of the Roman Empire and they looked very similar to the main headquarters of the governor and his staff in Cologne (on the Rhine in Western Germany). It began to look fairly certain that the palace of the Governor of Britain once stood on the Cannon Street Station site. The great halls would be used for meetings and official parties; the rows of small rooms must have been offices. The mosaics may have been part of the Governor's own private apartments. There were also the remains of a large pool with at least one fountain in it. Altogether it must have been a magnificent palace.

The Roman Governor was commander-in-chief of the army as well as head of the government. Most summers the Governor went on campaign with his soldiers, but all winter he was in London looking after the running of the country. He made sure that law and order were respected and that the roads were kept in good repair. His deputy, the Procurator, controlled the officials who collected taxes.

The Governor and the Procurator did not always see eye to eye. When Suetonius Paulinus wanted to punish the Britons after Boudicca's revolt, his Procurator, Julianus Classicianus, protested to the Emperor that this harsh treatment would only lead to more rebellions. Today we are reminded of him by his great tombstone which is now in the British Museum. Part of it was found in 1852 when Tower Hill underground station was being built. Another part came to light when the station was enlarged in 1935. Skilled restorers joined the two pieces to a matching block of stone to replace the missing part. In Wakefield Gardens on Tower Hill there is now a life-size statue of Classicianus near where the tombstone was found. Beside it stands a stone slab with a copy of the inscription on the original tomb.

Classicianus' tomb. The inscription is Latin shorthand for 'To the spirits of the departed, and of Gaius Julius Alpinus Classicianus, son of Gaius, of the Fabian voting tribe, Procurator of the Province of Britain'. Underneath is the full name of his wife, who had the tomb made in his memory. You might expect such a large block to contain the body of the dead man, but Romans never buried their dead in the city. The bodies were either cremated or buried in cemeteries outside the walls.

The Fort

After Boudicca was defeated there were no more rebellions for many years. All the same, the Romans knew there was always a danger that the Britons might suddenly attack. They wanted to make sure that London could never again be caught by surprise.

The government decided to build a fort on the outskirts of the city so that there were always soldiers at hand to defend it. The site they chose was a little to the north-west of the centre of London: near enough to be on the spot at once if there was trouble, but not in the way of the private houses and shops.

Like the Governor's Palace, the fort has only been discovered quite recently. Bombing in the second world war destroyed the buildings which lay over it, and now you can see a length of its wall in Noble Street. The west gate of the fort is just north of London Wall; it is open most days at lunch-time.

Roman forts, even more than Roman towns, were built to a standard pattern. They were always the same shape, a rectangle with rounded corners like a playing card. Two roads ran from side to side in each direction, with a central square where they crossed. Today Wood Street runs along the line of the north/south road in London's fort, and Addle Street follows part of the line of the east/west road. The headquarters building stood beside the central square, with the commandant's house close by. Offices, a meeting hall, a small chapel and the strong room for the soldiers' pay were also nearby. In addition most forts had a hospital, stables, repair workshops and granaries.

Barracks for the soldiers to live in formed the main part of the fort. Again, there was a standard pattern. Each block held one century, the basic unit of the Roman army (originally one hundred men, but in practice nearer eighty). The centurion, who was the officer in charge, had several rooms at one end. The ordinary soldiers slept eight to a room. They kept their equipment in a smaller room alongside, and if the weather was fine they could sit out on the verandah to polish their swords and helmets.

Unlike modern soldiers, each Roman soldier preferred to cook his own food and there were outdoor ovens at each corner of the fort. They liked vegetables fried in fat, and a kind of thick porridge.

Shops and Town Hall

Most Londoners were shopkeepers and craftsmen, dockers and messengers. By now London was growing into a great trading city. Ships sailed up the Thames with cargoes from all over Europe. Some goods were sent straight away to customers in other parts of Britain. Many things stayed in London; more Romans lived here than in any other city in the country. They all wanted olive oil for their cooking and wine to drink. These were imported from France and Italy in tall pottery jars called 'amphora'. Rich Romans wanted clothes and jewellery, furniture and pottery, and the most fashionable came straight from Italy. Poorer people were content with the goods made by the craftsmen working in London which were cheaper.

The forum was the real centre of the city for both rich and poor. Every Roman town had a forum or market place at its centre with covered ways and permanent shops round three sides and market stalls in the middle. The fourth side was always the basilica or town hall.

There is still a market on the site of London's forum, though all the Roman buildings above ground level have disappeared. Today the whole of the market is under cover. It is called Leadenhall Market and is most famous for its meat.

A Roman foot soldier. The men stationed in London's fort would look like this. On campaign they would carry even more equipment.

The Forum and Basilica as they may have looked in 150 AD London's basilica was unusually large; it was 500 feet long, the same as St Paul's Cathedral. The offices for the local officials lay behind the main assembly hall.

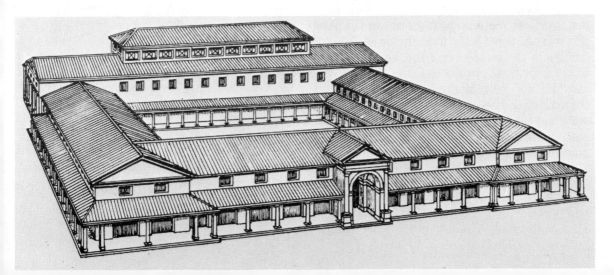

A butcher's shop, from a carving on a monument. Cleavers like this are still used by butchers, and so are massive chopping blocks. Many Roman craftsmen's tools were just the same shape as their present-day versions.

Before refrigerators were invented, all city dwellers shopped for every meal. Fresh fruit and vegetables, meat and fish, butter and eggs, were brought in daily from the country outside. They were laid out on folding tables and weighed on a portable balance.

Londoners tended to buy most of their food at the smaller, local markets. But for more expensive things like clothes, pots and pans, pottery and jewellery, they usually went to the forum.

At home in Italy the Romans had been used to meeting their friends in the forum. People liked to stop and gossip in the sunshine, often sitting down for a drink together while they told each other the latest news. It was not so tempting to linger like this on a cold, damp day in London. All the same, the Romans built all their forums in the same shape as those in Italy.

Homes

Roman shops stretched a long way back from the street. At the very back (or above the shop if it was two floors high) lived the owner and his family. In the middle came the workroom, and in the front there was the shop itself. The customer did not walk in through a door, or peer through plate glass windows. Instead, the goods were laid out on an open counter, just as they are still in some greengrocers and fishmongers. To shut the shop at night, the owner put up wooden shutters and barred them on the inside.

There were shops and homes like this all over London. One district was specially well-known for the fine craftsmen who worked there: this was the banks of the Wal Brook. Many tools and pieces of finely made metal have been dug up there.

There is another way of finding out what these shops looked like. Some monuments in Roman cities show carvings of different types of shop.

Though many Londoners lived above or behind their shops and workrooms, the richer families had elegant villas. The richest of all lived in large mansions, with the rooms arranged round a central courtyard. Such a house was dug up in Lower Thames Street, close by the river. The owner was so rich that he had his own suite of bath rooms. Part of this has survived, including the pillars which supported the floor. Slaves kept the furnace well stoked at the side of the house. The hot air circulated under the floor and up through small side openings into the room above.

The dining-room was usually the grandest room in a house like this. Here the Romans laid their finest floors, made of mosaic. Since these were made of thousands of fragments of stone, they lasted much longer than wooden floors.

Mosaic found in Leadenhall Street. Bacchus, the God of wine, riding on a panther. It was part of the floor of a large room, probably in a rich man's villa.

Even so, only a few small floors have managed to survive all the many rebuildings of London. Two are in the Bank of England, and special permission is needed to see them. Another is in a private office building. But it is easy to see the mosaic found in Leadenhall Street and now on show at the British Museum.

A wealthy Roman household needed a great many servants, and they lived in a special wing of the villa. Slaves kept the furnaces stoked to heat the main rooms and kept the charcoal cooking stoves alight. Others cleaned, filled and lit the oil lamps. Clothes were made and washed by hand.

Baths

The richer Romans had plenty of spare time. A favourite way to spend it was to visit the public baths. Both men and women could go, but at separate times or on different days. Poor people went too, since all the Romans thought it was very important to have frequent baths. Most Romans went to the public baths every day, not just for a wash but also to meet their friends. Some people joined in games in the exercise yard, others chatted with their friends while they moved from room to room.

Roman public baths were completely different from swimming pools today. They consisted of a series of rooms, each hotter than the last. Alongside the hottest room lay a furnace heating a tank of water to make steam (as in a modern Turkish bath). After you had taken off your clothes in the locker room, you passed into the coolest room. Next came the warm room, then the hot room and by then the bather's sweat was really flowing down him.

If you wanted, you could now ask a slave to rub your body with oil and then scrape you with a strigil. Then you could cool yourself down in the cool room, or jump in the pool and have a swim.

An artist's idea of the Public Baths in Cheapside. Notice the stokehole in the bottom left-hand corner, the wood pile, the exercise yard and the small outdoor pool.

A strigil and oil flask found in London. The strigil or scraper took off the dirt along with the oil, leaving the bather fresh and clean.

Although the public baths in London were small compared with the vast baths in Rome itself, they were quite elaborate. Two have been excavated, one in Upper Thames Street and one in Cheapside. Unfortunately they are not open to the public. The so-called Roman bath in Strand Lane is not genuine.

Sometimes the Roman wanted more entertainment than games and talk. Every town had an amphitheatre, a big oval stadium for prize fights and displays. A few towns also had a theatre. Up till now, no trace of either a theatre or an amphitheatre has been found in London. Yet it seems certain that a city as large as this would have had both; one day some clue will appear in a new excavation. All that has come to light so far is a statue of a gladiator, and we know that gladiator fights were popular in Roman amphitheatres. At the moment the nearest Roman theatre is at Verulamium, and the best remaining amphitheatre is further still, at Caerleon.

Temples

Another public building which has not yet been found is the temple to the Emperor. We know that other Roman towns had such temples; Boudicca burnt the temple to Claudius at Colchester.

There were usually other temples as well since the Romans worshipped so many different gods. They were quite small with room only for the priest and several altars.

Head of Mithras.

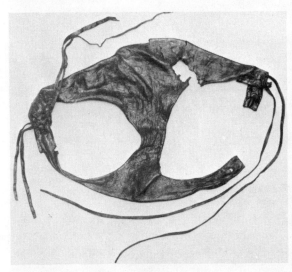

Pair of leather trunks found in a well. These briefs probably belonged to a dancer. She would wear them with a separate top, like a modern bikini.

The Walbrook Mithraeum. The Temple of Mithras rebuilt in Queen Victoria Street. You can see the bases of the columns, and the bay or apse at the far end where the altars stood.

For a long time no temple ruins of any kind were found. Then in 1953 the outline of a temple to Mithras came to light while foundations were being dug for a large office block in Bucklersbury. The stones were relaid by the side of the street in front of the new building in Queen Victoria Street so that the public could see them easily.

Mithras was a Persian god. Soldiers who had fought in the East had worshipped this god and brought their new religion to Britain. Mithras was thought to approve of courage, strength and fair play, and this was why soldiers were specially keen on his worship.

Unusually, the temple to Mithras provided room for the congregation to sit while they took part in the service. There was an apse at one end where the altars stood and archaeologists dug up several statues on this spot. The biggest was a head of the god Mithras himself—he is wearing the Phrygian cap which is his special badge.

This temple to Mithras was built towards the end of the second century AD, when Roman London was at its height. The population was somewhere near 50 000 and the city was thriving. Unhappily, other parts of the Roman Empire were not doing so well. On the northern borders, especially in Germany and along Hadrian's Wall, there was constant fighting. Some of the tribes living outside the empire took to making quick raids on the coast of Britain.

The Wall

Altogether it was not a very peaceful time. About 190 AD the government decided to build a wall round London to stop an attack by raiders from the coast. It would also be useful if civil war broke out.

Stone was ordered from the Kent quarries, and hundreds of boatloads went down the river Medway to the Thames estuary. They sailed up the Thames and unloaded at the docks above and below London Bridge. One boat sank before the stone could be got off her; she was found on the river bed near Blackfriars Bridge in 1962.

A huge wall, two and a half miles long, was built all round London. It ran from the river bank near Blackfriars, round all the built-up area, and down to the river again where the Tower now stands. The wall was twenty feet (six metres) high and tapered up from a broad

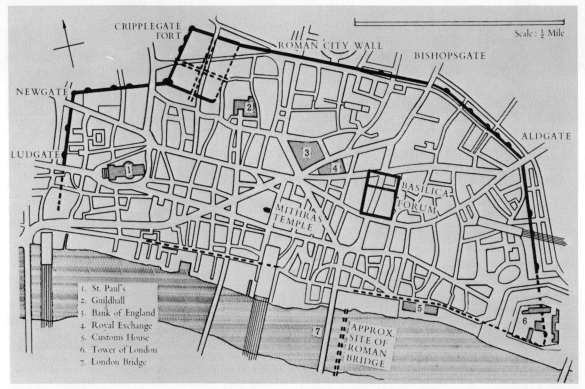

The City of London showing the Roman wall and principal buildings in relation to today's streets.

1. St. Paul's
2. Guildhall
3. Bank of England
4. Royal Exchange
5. Customs House
6. Tower of London
7. London Bridge

base to a parapet wide enough to walk along comfortably. Just beyond it, a ditch was dug. Separate bands of red tile were inserted in the stone to give extra strength.

Little of the wall still survives. Yet all through the middle ages it was kept in good repair, while Londoners still needed its protection. This means that the upper sections of the wall that is left are medieval, not Roman. You can usually tell where the later parts begin because small, more uneven stones were used.

The three best places to see the wall are: in Wakefield Gardens, by Tower Hill underground station; behind a modern office block in Cooper's Row, opposite Trinity House; and in St Alphege's church yard, beside the new road called London Wall.

If you put a wall round a city, you must also build gates. There are no traces of them today, except for part of one gate of the fort. Yet we know exactly where each gate stood, since they have all given their names to the roads which went through them.

Four stood where main roads entered London from Colchester, York, Chester and Silchester. Two more were originally the north and west gates of the fort. The seventh, Aldersgate, stood where a small local road entered the city. Remembering the names ending in '–gate' which you looked for early in this book, you may be asking 'What about Moorgate?' It lies on the line of the Roman wall, but was only built in the middle ages.

Archaeologists have tried to work out what these gates looked like, using the few remains that have come to light during recent rebuilding. They have also used their knowledge of better preserved gates in other cities; the Porta Nigra in Trier (West Germany) is a good example. All main gates had double entrances: traffic entering the town used one door, while those leaving went out by the other door. Beside and above the gates were the guards' quarters. Someone was always on duty to see that no enemy came in, and to close the doors at night.

Newgate is the one we know most about. It had two large square turrets and the road leading up to it was twelve yards wide. Other gates may have had rounded towers like the ones at Trier.

The troubled times did not end after the wall was built. Londoners may have felt safer, but in other parts of the Roman Empire people were in great danger. The tribes beyond the frontiers made more daring attacks. Sea raiders from North Germany made lightning swoops on the south and east coasts of Britain despite a line of forts which were built to scare them away.

Emperors and generals fought each other for power. One soldier called Carausius had the nerve to call himself Emperor of Britain but he was soon murdered by a rival, Allectus. Not long afterwards, the true Emperor arrived from Rome to restore peace. His name was Constantius Chlorus. He sailed up the Thames and reached London just in time to stop the rebel soldiers looting the city. To celebrate his arrival and his success, he ordered a gold medal to be made.

As the Emperors spent more and more time fighting each other, the soldiers lost their loyalty to Rome. It was no longer a glorious empire to fight for, and the men began to get slack and lazy. Meanwhile the barbarians grew bolder. Instead of just making quick raids, they crossed the frontiers in whole armies and began to stay. A great many troops were called back from Britain to defend Italy. Soon one of the fiercest barbarian tribes, the Goths, was threatening Rome itself. This terrible news reached the few Roman soldiers left in Britain in 410 AD. Orders came that they must pack their belongings and hurry home. Now that the whole Empire was crumbling, there were no forces to spare for a remote province like Britain.

No one knows exactly how many Romans stayed behind after the soldiers had gone. Nor do we know how long they kept up the Roman way of life. Historians used to think that London was left completely empty for a while. But now it is beginning to look as if it was never abandoned altogether. A few Romans stayed on in the almost empty city, possibly joined by Britons who liked the Roman way of living. Although the public buildings gradually fell into ruins, some sort of life went on.

Constantius Chlorus' medal. A woman is kneeling beside the city gate to welcome the Emperor, and you can see the letters LON written below her. Presumably Constantius has just arrived in the boat shown at the foot of the medal.

Questions on Roman London

1 Why was the site of London a specially good place for a capital city to develop?

2 Tell the story of Boudicca's attack on London from the point of view of *either* an Iceni tribesman *or* a Roman soldier.

3 Choose an object made by a Roman craftsman; draw it; then describe how a Roman went shopping in London's forum to buy it.

4 Use your library to find out more about the daily life of a soldier in the fort. What was his barracks like? What did he wear? What did he eat?

5 Make up a work schedule for a team building London's wall. Where do they collect their materials? What would a working diagram look like? What digging has to be done before the stones are laid?

6 The year is 410 AD. A Roman family living in London has to decide whether to go back to Italy or stay on in Britain. Make up the argument that might have taken place between members of the family.

From Roman to Medieval

Most of the buildings seem to have been left empty. Soon roofs fell in, floorboards rotted and wells were choked with rubbish.

The invading Angles and Saxons did not want to settle in towns. Instead, they came to Britain in search of rich farming land. Yet places which were in deep country at that time are now well within the built-up area of London. You will find plenty of places ending in 'ton', 'ing' or 'ham', which show they were started by Anglo-Saxons. Paddington, for example, means the farmstead of Padda and his people; Barking was the settlement of Berica's people. See how many place-names with these endings you can find on a modern map of the Greater London area.

As the Anglo-Saxons made themselves at home in their new country, towns revived. It was useful to have a place within an easy journey from your village where you could buy goods you could not make yourself. In a town travelling merchants could make contact with new customers by visiting the market.

When Christian missionaries reached England they found the towns were good centres to preach in. In 604 St Augustine made one of his followers, Mellitus, the first Bishop of London. Then the King of Kent built Mellitus a church on Ludgate Hill. This was the first St Paul's Cathedral.

Little by little traders from overseas started coming to London again. Merchant ships sailed up the Thames with fine goods from Europe, and filled their holds with English wool, cloth and corn for the journey back.

Just as London seemed to be coming to life again, fresh invaders arrived. Danes had been making daring raids on the north-east coast; then each year they started to come further south. Many Londoners were killed in a raid in 842. Nine years later the Danes came back and burnt the whole city. As in Boudicca's time it was all made of wood and caught alight easily.

Alfred, King of Wessex, was the first man to make a real stand against the Danes. By now the Danes had settled down to live in all the central part of England, and were hoping to take over the south as well. Alfred made up his mind to stop them. He drove them out of his own kingdom of Wessex; then, in 886, he captured London from them.

Alfred had London's walls mended and encouraged people to make their homes in the town. Each year more people came to enjoy the peace and safety which Alfred had brought.

Although London grew fast, it was not yet the capital of England. The country was divided into several kingdoms, and each had its own capital. The capital of Wessex was Winchester. Even when the kingdoms were joined together under one King of all England (Alfred's great-grandson, Edgar) Winchester remained the capital.

London's real strength came from its trade. When the Danes attacked again, a hundred years later, the citizens were now strong enough to fight them off and London only gave in when its leader suddenly died.

Eventually the Danish leader Cnut became King of England and merchants from his other Kingdoms (Norway and Denmark) came to trade peacefully in London. Cnut was strong enough to win trading rights for London merchants in other European countries as well.

Many Danes made their homes in London. St Clement Danes Church stands near one of their settlements. Another group lived at Haakon's Island (which we call Hackney). A church in Southwark and several others were called after St Olaf, a favourite Norwegian saint.

When the last of Cnut's sons died leaving no heir, Edward the Confessor became King. He belonged to the old English royal family which descended from Alfred. Edward was crowned at Winchester. It was still the capital, though by now London was the larger and richer city.

Edward's great gift to London was Westminster Abbey. When he built his monastery by the Thames, it lay two miles to the west of London itself, with open country in between.

The Abbey (the monastery church) was finished just before Edward died in January 1066. He was buried in it, and you can still see his tomb behind the high altar. Westminster Abbey's first coronation took place later the same day, when Harold was crowned King.

Westminster Abbey, as it is shown in the Bayeux Tapestry. The Latin inscription reads 'Here the body of King Edward is carried to the church of St Peter'. The abbey looks very different today because it was rebuilt in the 13th century.

Only ten months later Harold was dead. The Normans had invaded and beaten the English at Hastings. William of Normandy captured London soon after and made himself king.

With the arrival of the Normans London was firmly established as the capital of England. During the middle ages it grew to be one of the greatest cities in Europe. The wooden buildings were largely replaced with stone. The city got its own mayor and Common Council and became self-governing. All this forms the next part of London's story.

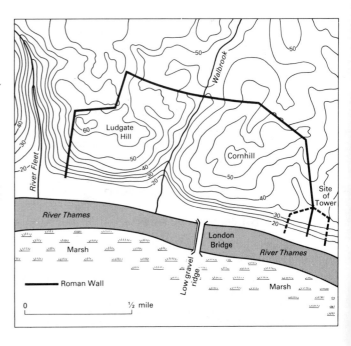

The site of the city of London. This map shows where the Romans built their wall and the position of London Bridge. The Tower of London was built at the eastern end of the wall. (See especially pp. 6 and 7.)

2
Medieval London

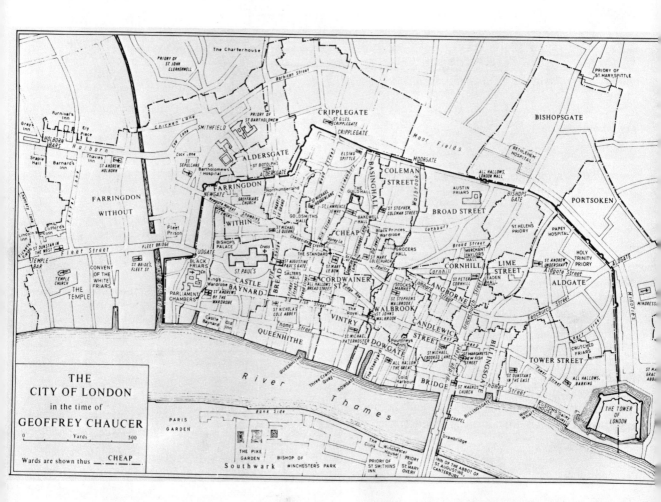

Map of Medieval London, showing the 24 wards of the City. (Geffrey Chaucer lived 1349-1400)

The Shape of the City

If you look at a map of medieval London, the first thing you notice is that the line of the wall has not changed since Roman times. But the built-up area has spilt beyond the walls (especially to the west) and the position of the streets has completely changed. When the Roman buildings fell to ruin, the stones and tiles were not cleared away. New streets and houses were built on top of the rubbish, when and where they were needed; there was no plan. There were only a few fairly straight roads across from side to side. A twisted network of little streets and alleys grew up in between.

The population more than doubled in the 200 years from William I to Edward I. This meant that more and more homes were needed.

Most were made of wood, which was simple and quick to use. First you put up a wooden frame, then made walls by filling in the spaces with woven twigs daubed with mud and plaster.

In spite of the growing population, there were still plenty of gardens. The bishops of Ely even had a vineyard in their large garden at Ely Place. Most backyards had some room for flowers.

A number of Londoners had country jobs. When the bell of St Mary le Bow rang each evening for the curfew, gardeners and labourers streamed in through the gates from the fields outside.

The new Londoners came from all over England and beyond. Some were from Normandy, like Thomas à Becket's father. The poet Chaucer was the grandson of an Ipswich man. Dick Whittington's father was a squire in Gloucestershire. London was the place to come if you wanted to rise quickly in the world and make a lot of money.

But many visitors coming for the first time were not so impressed. They were shocked by the noise, the crowds and the danger. Stallholders would pester you, shouting out and thrusting their wares under your nose.

Westminster was growing too. All the government departments made their headquarters here. When Parliaments were first called in the thirteenth century, they met in the Palace of Westminster. The Common Law Courts were held in Westminster Hall. (*See next page.*)

By the end of the middle ages London and Westminster were no longer two separate places; London was truly England's capital.

Norman London and the Building of the Tower

The Tower of London is the largest of all the buildings in the City which remain from the Middle Ages. The centre part, the White Tower, is also one of the oldest. After William of Normandy had beaten the English at Hastings in 1066, he came to London. It was already the biggest town in England, though Winchester was still the capital. William was crowned king in Westminster Abbey on Christmas Day, 1066. The Londoners waiting outside raised such a shout

that the Normans thought a riot was starting! Soldiers rushed out to keep order and several people got killed, all for nothing.

William wanted to make sure he had a really firm hold on London. Straight away he made his soldiers build an earth mound with a wooden castle on top. This would give him and his family somewhere safe to live in case there was a revolt. His mound (or motte) was in the south-east corner of the city, just beside where the Tower was later built.

The Normans built mottes like this all over England, so that their small army could control the whole country. Many were later converted into stone keeps or square castles. The White Tower is one of them.

William ordered a French monk called Gundulf to take charge of the building of the Tower in 1078. It was three storeys high, built roughly square with four corner turrets. The walls were really thick: fifteen feet (5 metres) at the bottom and eleven (nearly 4 metres) at the top. On each floor there was a very big hall and a smaller hall.

The Tower in the 15th century. Look for London Bridge and the spires of City churches at the top of the picture. The grassy slope on the right is Tower Hill.

The Tower and Tower Bridge viewed from the air. The White Tower stands surrounded by later additions. You can see the rounded end of the Chapel of St John, and Traitors' gate. Tower Bridge was not built until the end of the 19th century.

The rest of the space was filled by a chapel. Down in the basement came store-rooms, dungeons and a well. The royal family had its private rooms on the top floor. Below this there were rooms for soldiers and members of the Court.

William also built two smaller castles on the west side of London, Baynard's Castle and Mountfitchet Tower. No other defences were needed as the old Roman wall was still there. As long as it was kept mended and had new stones added along the top, it served very well.

William I's son, William Rufus, preferred Westminster. He built Westminster Hall which is close by the Abbey, and is still standing. He added rooms to the palace Edward the Confessor had started, making a more comfortable place to live than the stark Tower of London.

All the same, the King and his family went on using the Tower from time to time all through the middle ages. It was the strongest and safest place in the City.

Castle design changed as time passed, and the Tower had to be brought up to date. By the late thirteenth century castles were being built in two layers: an inner keep and an outer ring of strong towers linked by high walls. The White Tower provided the inner keep, but an outer ring was needed. The first of the new towers was added in Edward I's time. In the end there were thirteen towers in this outer ring, and a wide moat beyond them. If you go to the Tower and buy a guide book it will give you details of each of these towers.

Two at least, the Beauchamp Tower and the Bloody Tower, were used as state prisons. You can go inside and see the mottoes and initials carved on the walls by the prisoners. All were accused of treason. If they arrived by river, they came into the Tower through Traitors' Gate. Many did not come out again alive.

In the Bloody Tower you can see the winding gear for the grid or portcullis which could be let down as an extra door. In fact you had to go through two sets of gate towers if you wanted to enter the Tower by land. Altogether it was a difficult place for an enemy to capture.

The Tower must often have seemed a grim place to the citizens of London. Many executions took place on Tower Hill just to the north, as well as the executions in the Tower itself. Yet there was fun there too, as it was the home of the royal zoo. Only the ravens are left, but once there were all kinds of animals. The King of France sent an elephant to Henry III in 1255. It was the first one in England, and a special house had to be built for it in the Tower grounds.

Londoners' Leisure

Londoners had plenty of ways of spending their spare time besides watching the King's animals. William Fitzstephen, who lived in the twelfth century, wrote proudly about all the sports they could enjoy.

Each Shrove Tuesday the boys had time off school to watch cock-fighting. That same afternoon they all went out into the fields to play football. Boys from each school came with their own ball; so did the young apprentices from each craft. Plenty of older men went along too to watch the matches.

On Sundays in Lent jousting was popular. Young men rode out of the city after dinner to have mock battles on horseback. They used spears with blunt points so that no one got hurt.

With the warmer weather at Easter time, water sports began. A shield was firmly tied to a pole in the middle of the river, by London Bridge. Then a group of boys rowed a boat towards it, while one of them stood at the prow with a lance held ready. He tried to aim his lance plumb in the middle of the shield so that it split. Crowds watching on the bridge often saw a boy miss his aim, lose his balance and fall in the water. But there were always several boats standing by ready to fish him out!

All through the summer the boys would be out in the fields on every free day. There were jumping and wrestling matches, archery and throwing the javelin.

When winter came the great marsh just to the north of the city often froze over. Fitzstephen wrote that great crowds of youths went out to have fun on the ice. 'Some gathering speed by a run, glide sidelong, with feet set well apart, over vast spaces of ice. Others make themselves seats of ice like millstones and are dragged along.' Others, more skilled, made themselves skates out of mutton bones and tied them under their shoes so that they could skim over the ice at high speed.

Though the city was growing fast, you could still get out quickly into open country. Fitzstephen tells us that Londoners were allowed to hunt in the forests round the city. Some went out with falcons; others took dogs with them to hunt the deer.

However late you got back, you could always find a hot meal. Fitzstephen was specially proud of the public cookshop down by the edge of the river. Here you could come at any hour and either eat a meal straight away or have it wrapped up to take home with you.

London Bridge

During King Henry II's reign, in 1176, it was decided to make a bridge in stone at the place where the Romans had erected their bridge. The King put a tax on wool to raise money to pay for it (starting a legend that the bridge rests on bags of wool).

Peter of Colechurch was given the job of Bridge Master. It was a huge job and took thirty years to finish. In the end it was 900 ft long and 20 ft wide (273 × 6 metres). Several people lost their lives, drowned as they worked to sink the twenty piers on which the bridge rested. These piers were not evenly spaced; some of the gaps were much wider than others, to leave room for boats to sail through. Even so, it was always a risky place to pass because of the rapid flow of the water.

Tall boats could not sail under the bridge. So a space was left for them to go through, normally covered by a drawbridge. Just beside this stood

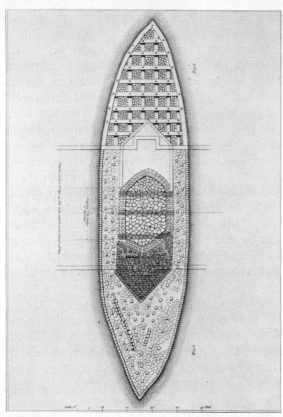

A Starling from London Bridge. The bridge was supported by twenty 'starlings' like this. The base of each one is a ring of stout wooden posts filled with broken stones. Outside there is a boat-shaped platform made of wooden piles.

Drawbridge Gate. At the southern end of the bridge there was another gate called Stone Gate. Both of these could be shut to keep out unwanted people. Several times rebels trying to get into London were halted for a while because the bridge gates were closed against them.

Houses stood all along the bridge, although it was so narrow. They jutted right out over the river on one side, and over the road on the other. In several places the houses met in the middle so that the road seemed to pass through a tunnel.

Right in the centre of the bridge was the chapel of St Thomas à Becket. Peter Colechurch had once been the chaplain of the church where Becket was christened; he started to build the bridge only six years after Becket's murder. It was for these reasons that he chose to name the bridge chapel after Thomas. Later the bridge became the first stage on a London pilgrim's journey to Thomas' shrine at Canterbury. Just over the bridge the pilgrims all gathered at the Tabard Inn in Southwark, ready to start their pilgrimage.

This same stone bridge with its twenty 'starlings' (supports), was mended many times but it lasted nearly 700 years, right up till 1832. For most of that time it was the only bridge in London.

Trade and Shops

London had many gardens and orchards all through the middle ages. Some of the citizens also owned fields outside the walls where they could grow food. But for a great city like this the bulk of the food had to be brought in from outside. There were shops all over the town, and several markets.

Everyone needed bread. Only one street was actually called Bread Street, but many had bakers' shops in them. Some were owned by rich corn merchants who saw there was always plenty of flour.

Meat came in from the countryside around, and fish from the sea ports. In winter the meat would be salted and not very pleasant to eat. Much of the fish was dried or salted too. Everyone ate fish on Fridays and all during Lent.

A fish stall. Medieval Londoners bought much of their food at open stalls like this. Notice the scales, and the weights in the man's hand.

There were always chickens and rabbits to make a change of taste; many citizens kept pigs in their back yards.

If you wanted to buy meat, there were two specially good places to shop. One was the row of butchers' shops just inside Newgate; the other was the Stocks, a meat and fish market where the Mansion House now stands. If you fancied a plump chicken for dinner, you might go to the street called the Poultry.

All sorts of daily shopping could be done at the stalls set up each morning in the extra wide streets of East and West Cheap. But if you wanted something bigger you usually went to a craftsman's shop.

Here the name of the street often helped you find what you wanted. A gold ring could be bought in Goldsmith's Row. You could order a leather coat in Skinner's Lane. Most trades gathered in one particular street or area in this way. Everyone knew that you went to Foster Lane for a saddle or to Candlewick Street for cloth, though in these cases the name did not help.

Not all the London merchants had shops. Many of the richest men were wholesalers; they dealt with huge orders, often from other countries.

London had a busy trade with the Baltic. Quantities of furs were shipped in, mainly sable, ermine and gris (grey squirrel). Beaver was a common animal in Europe in medieval times, and a great many pelts were imported.

Fine leather arrived from Spain for gloves and shoes. The men who worked it, the Cordwainers, were named after the Spanish town of Cordova. Wine from France was unloaded at a quay called the Vintry by the mouth of the Walbrook. German merchants brought their special white wine called Hock. They also had fine cloth, gold and silver cups and jewellery in their ships.

These German merchants were specially successful. They brought in more and more luxury goods, and even grain if there was a bad harvest. The City gave them an area by the Thames as their headquarters, called the Steelyard. Here they had their own docks, warehouses and private homes. In return the German merchants (often called the Hanseatic men) promised to keep Bishopsgate in good repair.

Medieval ship. Rich wool merchants often owned their own ships; broad-based ones like this were known as 'cogs'. The wool was loaded on at the quays below London Bridge for its journey across the Channel.

Italians also came to do trade with Londoners. Bankers from the part of North Italy called Lombardy have given their name to Lombard Street.

As time went on, the biggest trade of all was in wool and all the imports mentioned above were paid for in wool or cloth. The weavers of Flanders (now part of Belgium and northern France) had so many orders for cloth that they needed to buy raw wool from outside. English sheep grew specially good wool, and many English merchants made fortunes by organizing its sale. Most of it was shipped out from London to Calais.

Only one of the rich merchants' houses has survived, and even that is no longer on the

Inside Crosby Hall, on Chelsea Embankment. The original site in Bishopsgate is marked by a plaque. The Great Hall stood on one side of a courtyard, which was reached through a gatehouse from the street.

same site. This is Crosby Hall, home of Sir John Crosby who made his fortune as a draper. When he lived there it stood in Bishopsgate. In fact you can see his tomb in the nearby church of St Helen's, Bishopsgate. But in 1910 the great hall of his mansion was moved to Chelsea to make room for new office buildings. You can see the outside of it from Cheyne Walk. Inside you are struck by the length and height of the hall. The roof is the finest part of all, with the ribs and bosses picked out in red, blue and gold. Sir John was very rich indeed.

The Government of London

Many of the rich merchants, like Sir John Crosby, took an active part in their trade or craft. The Lord Mayor of London was chosen from among them each year.

Yet London did not always have a mayor, or even the right to run its own affairs. All its rights were won after hard struggles with the king, or after quarrels between different groups of citizens.

Long before she had a mayor, London had a Folkmoot. This was a meeting of all the citizens and it took place three times a year. A bell rang, and all the citizens gathered at St Paul's Cross, close by the Cathedral.

There was also a Husting from very early times. This was the main court of law for the City, and it met once a week. To make sure that the law was obeyed in every part of the City, aldermen were chosen. There was one alderman for each ward; in the middle ages London was divided into twenty-four wards (in the City now there are twenty-six).

The aldermen did most of the work involved in the every-day running of the City. As the work grew, they wanted the citizens to take a share in it. This led to the calling of the Common Council; up to four members came from each ward.

All through the twelfth century London was growing particularly fast. The leading citizens began to want even more share in running their own affairs. They did not like to be told what to do by the Sheriffs, who were officials chosen by the King. They wanted to have their own men in charge.

Their chance came while Richard I was away fighting in the crusades. Richard's younger brother, John, wanted the citizen's support against the man who was ruling England on Richard's behalf.

The citizens agreed to help him—on one condition: that John would grant them a commune. Just at this time, 'communes' (groups of citizens running a town's affairs) were being set up in many parts of Europe. Londoners took the commune of Rouen, in northern France, as their model. They set up a council of important citizens and chose a mayor to lead it. At the same time, men from the newer, less wealthy crafts now got a share of power. You find skinners, fishmongers, corders (rope makers) and members of several other trades becoming aldermen for the first time.

London's first mayor was called Henry Fitz-Ailwin. He was chosen for life in 1192. When John was later forced to agree to Magna Carta, one item confirmed the Londoners' right to elect a mayor each year. That is still the practice today.

You might think all would go smoothly now, with a Council and a mayor in charge. But other kings were keen to win back control of London. Henry III accused the mayor and some of the aldermen of taking bribes, and had them sacked.

London lost the right to run her own affairs for many years. She did not get it back till Royal Charters were given to her in Edward II's reign. The new mayor has been elected by the aldermen every autumn without a gap from that time onwards. It started by being on 28 October, now it is 29 September.

The mayor became the chief authority in the City, and the man who stood for the whole city in the eyes of the outside world. He was given a guard of honour and a personal sword bearer. After his election the new mayor took an oath at Westminster. Straight after that the Lord Mayor's show took place. Like today, it was a brilliant free

The second seal for the Mayors of London, made in 1381. St Thomas Becket and St Paul are shown, with the City's arms underneath.

show for Londoners; colourful carts were pulled through the streets, plays and music were put on. In the middle ages it ended with a banquet in the mayor's own house. Today there are far too many guests for that, so it takes place in the Guildhall.

The city's population went on growing, and more and more houses were built outside the walls. The wards had to be made larger to include these new citizens. The new part of a ward beyond the wall was called 'Without'. For example, there is Faringdon ward within and Faringdon ward without, side by side. The poll tax, which had to be paid by every household, shows that there were between 35 000 and 40 000 Londoners by 1377.

The mayor and aldermen tried to control the bad side of this quick growth. For example, fires were always breaking out in the close-crammed wooden houses. So a rule was made that at least the walls between the houses should be built of stone, and roofs should be tiled, not thatched. The same rule was repeated year after year, so one must presume that a lot of people took no notice of it.

Citizens also disobeyed the rule forbidding them to allow their pigs to roam the streets. Only one owner's pigs were allowed to wander—those belonging to St Anthony's Hospital in Thread-needle Street. Here monks nursed people suffering from rye-bread poisoning, a very common and unpleasant illness in the middle ages. It was usually known as St Anthony's Fire. Pigs became the hospital's mascots because St Anthony dreamt he fought and overcame a pig who was a symbol for Greed. Later, when part of the hospital became a school, the boys were nick-named St Anthony's pigs!

It was always a struggle to keep the streets clean. People poured their slops and rubbish into an open drain running down the middle of the street. There was only one public lavatory, at Queenhithe. Otherwise men used any odd corner, and citizens complained that the streets stank. Each ward had four rubbish collectors and four pig catchers; it was not enough. By the 1460s the river Walbrook was so foul that it had to be cleaned out and covered over.

Water supply became a problem too. In 1237

the City bought the wells at Tyburn from a private citizen. They built a reservoir, and laid a pipe from there to a pump in Cheapside. Very rich people could pay to have their own pipe leading off it to their house.

The Guildhall

The name of London's Town Hall, the Guildhall, reminds us that the city was run by men belonging to the great crafts, or guilds. Instead of standing proudly in a public square, Guildhall is almost

The Crypt of the Guildhall. This lies underneath the main hall, and is one of the oldest parts of the building.

hidden from the street. You go into a courtyard past the church of St Lawrence Jewry, now the Corporation church.

There was probably a small hall here in the early middle ages. By 1411, though, the Common Council decided that London deserved a fine new hall. Some rich citizens offered to pay for different parts of the building. Dick Whittington, for example, provided glass for the windows and marble for the floor. Today only the walls of the original hall are left; it has had several new roofs and new fronts. Yet it still has the look of a great medieval hall. Kitchens were added in 1501 so that official dinners could be held here.

As well as the Guildhall, each craft guild had its own hall. Only one survives from the middle

ages (and then only a small part)—the Merchant Taylors' hall.

Today you do not really have to be a tailor to belong to the Merchant Tailors, or a leather worker to belong to the Skinners. The old working craft guilds have turned into today's City Livery Companies. But the companies still take care of their members, and other people in need. Some of them run schools, most have almshouses for old people. You have to belong to one of the City Companies to become an alderman or Lord Mayor.

London's Churches

Today the city's churches are much smaller than the huge office blocks which tower over them. But in the middle ages (and right on till the second world war) they were the tallest and most striking buildings in London.

The biggest of all was St Paul's Cathedral. This was not the great domed building which we have today, but a medieval church with pointed windows.

It was like a parish church for the whole city, holding big services of remembrance and thanksgiving. In the middle ages it was used as a general meeting place as well, since it was by far the largest public hall in the city. It was 585 feet long, even longer than our St Paul's. With its 450 foot spire it was also taller than today's dome.

In the middle ages no one thought of churches as places you only visited on Sundays. In every parish the church was the local public hall and the centre of social life. Plays were held here; business men met to deal in the church porch. It was used for parties and meetings of every kind.

London in the fourteenth century had over 100 parish churches, more than any other town in Western Europe. Londoners liked to have a small local church within a few minutes' walk from where they lived. They might drop in for quiet prayer on a week day as well as attending several services each Sunday.

London grew quickly in the eleventh and twelfth centuries. People quite often found they had money to spare and where the neighbourhood did not have its own parish church, they might think of starting one. Either they persuaded some friends to join in the venture, or if they were rich enough they might found one on their own. It was necessary for them to provide some land, pay for the building, and choose a priest to take the services.

At first there was no exact line between one parish and the next. But by the mid-twelfth century it was clearly much simpler if each citizen knew which parish he lived in. The boundaries drawn at that date have hardly changed since. They are so crooked that a map of them looks rather like a jigsaw puzzle. This is because the line often followed the edge of the founders' private property.

Each person in a parish had two rights: to have his children baptized in the church, and to be buried either in the church or the churchyard. In return, he paid a tax called the tithe to his parish priest. This paid for the upkeep of the church and the priest's food and clothing.

Each parish church is named after a saint or saints. The choice of name often tells us something about the man who founded it. St Mary Woolnoth (rebuilt in the eighteenth century) was probably named after its Norman founder Wulfnoth. There are several St Botolphs, and he is known to have been a saint much loved by

Inside old St Paul's Cathedral. This drawing was made in the 17th century, not long before the building was burnt down. The Cathedral had been completed in 1314.

people from East Anglia. He was also a patron saint of travellers. Find out if there are any St Botolph churches near London's gates.

St Andrew Undershaft (one of the few medieval churches still left) was named after the shaft of the maypole. This was set up every 1 May and kept in the church the rest of the year. The young people of the parish danced round it each May Day till 1517. In that year there was a riot on 'Evil May Day' and many people were killed. So the maypole was never set up again.

Most of London's medieval churches were burnt down in the Great Fire of 1666. Nearly all were rebuilt on the same site (but with a totally different design). Sometimes there are fragments of the old church underneath the new one. At All Hallows Barking, just by the Tower of London, there are several layers. The first All Hallows was founded by the nuns of Barking Abbey (several miles further east), for their tenants in the City. When the church was bombed in the Second World War, parts of the first little Saxon church were uncovered. In the middle ages a bigger church was needed, so side aisles were added and the choir was enlarged. Later still a tower was added, and a chapel down in the crypt.

Monasteries

While some rich men gave their money to build a parish church, others used theirs to found a monastery. London had many monasteries, nunneries and friaries, as well as its parish churches. Everyone must have been used to the sound of bells ringing for services.

If you decided to start a monastery, you needed a larger piece of land than for a parish church. First a chapel had to be built where the monks or nuns went for services. These were held several times a day, beginning in the very early morning. They also needed a dormitory to sleep in, a refectory to eat in, an infirmary for the old and sick, and a cloister to work in.

Very few of the buildings where the monks and nuns lived are still standing. When Henry VIII closed the monasteries many were pulled down or adapted for a different use. But several of the chapels have survived, usually because they were taken over as parish churches.

St Bartholomew the Great was one of the biggest. The part you see today was only the choir of the monastery chapel, so the whole thing must have been huge. The cloisters were nearly lost as well. They were turned into stables, and only mended and given back to the church early this century.

St Bartholomew's is one of the only Norman churches left in London. You can always spot Norman work by the round arches and heavy pillars. Here the semi-circle of arches behind the altar was built to give the monks room to walk in procession on feast days.

The monks of St Bartholomew's Priory had special work to do. Its founder, Rahere, had started St Bartholomew's Hospital alongside the monastery for the poor and sick of London. Rahere was court jester to Henry I, but a dream had changed his life. Once, as he lay desperately ill, St Bartholomew had appeared to him; Rahere promised that if he got better, he would start a hospital. So 'Barts', the great hospital that stands by Smithfield meat market today, is the result of that vow.

Several of the London monasteries had hospitals attached. St Katharine's, beyond the Tower, ran one for old people. St Giles-in-the-Fields and St James's were both leper hospitals. Another, St Mary Spital, gave its name to a whole district: Spitalfields.

The nunnery of St Helen's, Bishopsgate, had its nuns' chapel directly alongside the local parish church. Today the wall between has been pulled down, and the result is a double church. The nunnery had been founded by William, a goldsmith's son, in 1216. It became a favourite place for City fathers to choose for their daughters; in fact it was more like a smart boarding school than a nunnery. Although all the other buildings have been pulled down, you can work out where they once stood. There is a small road off Bishopsgate called Great St Helen's which covers part of the site. The Leathersellers' Hall, north-east of the church, has replaced the nuns' refectory. Nearby Mincing Lane is named after the 'minchuns' (a nick-name for nuns), since St Helen's owned houses here.

The nuns of St Helen's belonged to the Benedictine Order, like Barking Abbey. Another

City nunnery belonged to the order of St Clare of Assisi, called the Minoresses (a sister Order to the friars of St Francis). This gave its name to the street north of the Tower called the Minories.

Just to the west lay one of London's richest abbeys, Holy Trinity at Aldgate (sometimes called Christchurch). It had been given lands once owned by the City, and its priors were always aldermen of Portsoken Ward. It also had to keep the bridge over the Walbrook in good repair, since it lay on the monastery's land. There is a plaque on the wall of Mitre Square to explain that the cloister was once on this site.

The Charterhouse is much the most complete of London's former monasteries. It is also the most unusual, since it belonged to the Carthusian Order. These monks lived specially strict lives; each man spent all day by himself in his own little cottage or cell instead of sharing a common dormitory and refectory like the monks of the other Orders.

The Charterhouse lies north-east of Smithfield meat market, just off Aldersgate, and Charter-

Inside the Priory church of St Bartholomew the Great, showing Rahere's tomb. Rahere started to build his priory in 1123, but the tomb was made nearly 400 years later. Notice the difference in style between the arches of the church and the canopy of the tomb.

Wash-House Court in the Charterhouse. This was where the lay brothers lived. They did not take such strict vows as the monks themselves. Only one doorway remains of the Great Cloister where each monk had his separate cell.

house Square is named after it. When the Black Death struck England in 1348, so many people died that all the churchyards were filled up. Sir Walter Manny acted quickly and leased a big field just north of St Bartholomew's to provide an extra cemetery. To pray for all these dead souls, he decided to found a monastery close beside it. But it took so long to settle all the details that the monastery did not actually open till 1371. It was many years later still that the whole place was complete, with rooms for twenty-four monks arranged round a great cloister.

Now the Charterhouse is a home for old men, and is only open to visitors once a week. Visit it if you get the chance; its completeness gives you more of a feeling of medieval London than any other building in the whole city.

Monks and nuns spent most of their time within the walls of their abbeys. The friars, on the other hand, were active in visiting people's homes and preaching to ordinary working men and women. The Black Friars were the first to reach London (also called the Dominicans, after their Spanish founder, St Dominic). They settled in the area between Ludgate Hill and the Thames; Blackfriars Bridge is just beside it. Their church was specially long to provide room for everyone who came to listen to their famous sermons. It stood south of Carter Lane, but nothing is left except two street names: Blackfriars Lane and Friar Street.

The Grey Friars or Franciscans were the next to arrive. Londoners liked them at once, perhaps because the order took so much trouble to visit the poor and sick. The friars were given a piece of land just north of Newgate, and many gifts of money followed. Their chapel came to be called Christchurch, and it still stands in the little street called Greyfriars Passage.

More orders of friars followed, each leaving almost nothing today except their name. The Carmelites or Whitefriars have a street named after them running south from Fleet St to the river, west of St Bride's Church. *The News of the World* has its offices here, including a room which was once part of the Prior's house.

The Augustine Friars were given land to the west of Old Broad St. Here two streets are named after the shortened version of their order: Austin Friars. The friars of the Holy Cross had their name altered even more. Their street, Crutched Friars, lies beside Fenchurch Street Station.

In addition to the many churches and monasteries, nunneries and friaries, two orders of knights had big estates just outside the city boundaries. The Knights of St John of Jerusalem had their headquarters in Clerkenwell. They are back there today, in a newer building beside the old Gatehouse; you know them better under their modern name of the St John's Ambulance Brigade.

The Knights Templars owned the Temple, to the west of the City. Now it houses two Inns of Court, Middle Temple and Inner Temple, where half the barristers of London have their offices.

The biggest of all the monasteries was Westminster Abbey—though it lay outside London at

The round nave of the Temple Church. The churches of the Knights Templars were always round, like the Temple in Jerusalem. The Order had been started to help men wounded on the Crusades. A few of the knights had the honour of being buried in the church itself, and you can see their tombs here.

that date. In 1245 Henry III decided that a larger and grander church was needed. After all, this was where the kings of England were both crowned and buried. He admired the style in which French cathedrals were being built at that time. So he ordered his new church to be in the same 'Gothic' pattern, with a very tall roof and thin pointed windows.

Later abbots added more buildings for the monks. There was a new hall, where the Westminster School boys eat now, an infirmary and a chapter house. The cloister is the easiest to visit; you just go through a door from the Abbey itself.

All through the middle ages Westminster Abbey had open country on its western side. Today the open area in front of the west door of the Abbey is called the Sanctuary. Once this name had a real meaning. Criminals escaping justice were safe from arrest so long as they stayed there.

The Strand and the Peasants' Revolt

At the beginning of the middle ages there were fields on the way from London to Westminster. They were still two separate places, joined by a road along the north bank of the Thames called the Strand. At Charing Cross the road turned a sharp angle to match the bend in the river. Here stood one of the crosses put up by Edward I in memory of his much-loved wife, Eleanor. It is the last of the twelve crosses marking the places where her coffin rested on its journey from Lincoln to Westminster. The cross you see there today is a modern one, standing just in front of Charing Cross Station.

All along the Strand from here to the city stood great houses. The first belonged to the Hungerford family, remembered today in the name of the footbridge crossing the river to the Royal Festival Hall. Many of the others were the town houses of bishops and rich lords. Look for the street names marking their sites: Norfolk, Arundel, Essex, Exeter, Durham, Carlisle, Worcester, York, Buckingham and Salisbury.

The largest and most splendid of all these mansions along the Strand was the Savoy Palace. Once it belonged to Peter of Savoy, uncle to

The Chapter House of Westminster Abbey. Henry III rebuilt this as an eight-sided room with a slim central pillar. Much later it became the meeting place of the House of Commons for a short while.

Henry III's wife; now there is a well-known hotel on the site. But its most famous owner in the middle ages was John of Gaunt, Edward III's rich and haughty son. Poor men hated him, and when the peasants rebelled and came to London in 1381, they burnt down the Savoy Palace.

Richard II, John of Gaunt's nephew, was on the throne at the time this happened. The country people were so angry at the harsh way their lords treated them that they came to London to protest to the king. This is called the Peasants' Revolt.

Two great bands of peasants arrived here that summer, one from Kent and the other from Essex. The Kent rebels reached Southwark on Wednesday, 12 June. First they broke into the two prisons, pulling down the wooden buildings and setting the prisoners free. Next day they

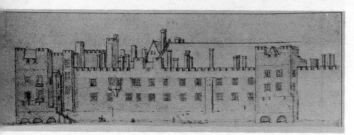

The Savoy Palace in the middle ages. Today the Savoy Hotel stands on part of the site.

tried to cross London Bridge to get into the city. But on the Mayor's orders, the bridge keeper pulled up the drawbridge. Then the people of Southwark sided with the peasants and threatened to kill the bridge keeper if he did not let it down again.

Now the Kent rebels poured across the bridge. Once in the city, they headed westwards. First they freed the prisoners in the Fleet prison. Then they broke into the Temple and grabbed the law books and charters from the lawyers' offices. The rebels piled them all into a great heap and set it alight. At last the hated rules (which bound the peasants to work for their lords) could never be read again.

Nearby the peasants found a cellar full of wine barrels. These were rolled out into the road, opened up and emptied down hundreds of thirsty throats. This gave the men new strength for the attack on their next target, the Savoy Palace. John of Gaunt was away on business in the north; but this did not save his palace. The peasants threw lighted torches among the clothes and bedding to set it on fire. Then they pushed three barrels onto the blaze, thinking they were filled with treasures. In fact they contained gunpowder. The fire roared up and spread till the whole mansion was ablaze.

Today all that is left of the Savoy Palace is its chapel, the Queen's Chapel of the Savoy. It lies in a little square just south of the Strand near Waterloo Bridge. The churchyard is a welcome patch of grass and trees among all the office and hotel buildings.

After attacking the palace, one group went off towards Westminster, setting alight several more houses on the way. But the great mass of rebels went to the Tower to try to speak to the King.

Richard II, who was only fourteen years old,

watched all that went on from a turret in the White Tower. He sent messengers to the Essex rebels, who had reached London in the meantime, to meet him at Mile End.

Here to the east of the city Richard listened patiently to the peasants' demands. Then he gave them charters freeing them from the need to work for their lords, just as they had hoped he would. The crowd now asked if they could seize anyone they believed to be a traitor. When the King agreed, they hurried off to the Tower. They knew that two much-hated men were hiding there—the Archbishop of Canterbury and the Lord Treasurer. They thought the Archbishop, as Chancellor, was ruling the country unjustly, while the Lord Treasurer had demanded a new and unpopular tax.

The Archbishop was praying in the Chapel of St John in the White Tower when the rebels burst in. This did not save him from being seized, and dragged along with the Lord Treasurer to Tower Hill. Here the two men, and several others, had their heads chopped off.

Again the King offered to meet the rebels. This time the men from Kent went to see him at Smithfield. Wat Tyler, the rebels' leader, rode straight up to the royal party. One account says that a courtier shouted out that Tyler was a liar. Furious at this insult, the rebel pulled out a dagger. At once the Lord Mayor hit him on the

The Murder of Wat Tyler. This picture shows two events from the Peasants' Revolt as if they were happening at the same time. On the left, the Lord Mayor is killing Wat Tyler, while Richard II looks on. To the right, the King is promising to grant the rebels' requests.

head; Tyler's dagger slid off the armour which the Lord Mayor wore under his tunic. Knights standing close by now rode forward and ran their swords at Tyler. He fell forward on the neck of his horse, stabbed to death.

The crowd of rebels were mad with anger at seeing their leader killed. They began to fit arrows to their bows. With great courage, Richard rode up to them and called out that he would lead them now and put all their troubles right. But he insisted that they went quietly home first. The peasants believed him and set off back to the country again. Once they were away from London, Richard's advisers told him to forget his promises.

Questions on Medieval London

1 Write down a list of four ways a young apprentice might have spent a winter day's holiday in medieval London.
2 Make a list of all the street names in the City of London which suggest a craft or a product.
3 How did London get its first Mayor? How is the Lord Mayor chosen today, and what is the name of the present one?
4 On an outline map of Europe draw in lines from London to all the countries with whom she traded. Write in the name of the goods imported along each line.
5 Imagine you hope to become a monk or friar in medieval London. What choice would you have? Find out about the different clothing, buildings and duties of the various Orders.
6 Draw the White Tower, and explain how and why it was built. Why was this site chosen?

The Dining Hall of Westminster School. This was originally the Abbot's hall. Queen Elizabeth refounded Westminster School to replace the school run by the monks.

The Closing of the Monasteries

If a Londoner had left the City in about 1530, and came back twenty years later, one change would have struck him above all the others. This was the disappearance of the monks and nuns and friars.

When he left, there would have been dozens of monasteries and nunneries in London, not to speak of the chantry chapels (where a priest said prayers for a dead man's soul). Yet when the Venetian ambassador described London in 1551, he wrote that there were 'many large palaces making a very fine show, but disfigured by the ruins of a multitude of churches and monasteries'.

Henry VIII had shut down all the monasteries in 1536–40, because they were very rich and corrupt and he badly needed money. Most of the buildings were sold to private buyers. The monks and nuns were given a small pension and turned out to find new homes.

Some of the new owners altered the building they had bought so as to turn it into a private house. Others pulled it down and used the stone to build somewhere else.

Sir Edward North had the pick of all the best monasteries in London; this was because he was in charge of selling them on the king's behalf. He chose the very finest for himself, the Charterhouse at Smithfield. Some of it could easily be turned into a private house, but he had no use for the church. So this was pulled down and the stone was used to build a big dining hall instead. The monks had eaten in a room that was so tall that North could fit a whole extra room in the upper part of it. Unfortunately he pulled down the great cloister with all the monks' separate cells leading off it. Queen Elizabeth probably saw it half-finished when she stayed here in 1558.

One monastery was never sold to a private owner. This was Greyfriars, near Smithfield, which was put straightaway to a useful purpose. The friars' chapel became a parish church; the other buildings were made into a home for 400 orphans, and given the name Christ's Hospital. By Edward VI's reign it had become a school as

well. The boys wore a long blue coat and yellow stockings (as they still do, though the school has moved out of London).

Some of the monasteries had cared for the poor and sick of London. People were sad to see them close, and the City persuaded Henry VIII to spare St Bartholomew's Hospital. The monks went away, but the Priory Church of St Bartholomew and the hospital were allowed to stay. Henry was not often so generous. He wanted the site of the leper hospital of St James, close to Whitehall. The hospital was pulled down and the King had a palace built there instead. When it was new, St James's Palace was in open fields. Now it is deep in central London, not far from Piccadilly.

In fact, Henry VIII had already found himself one new palace. When he sacked his chief minister, Cardinal Wolsey, he took over Wolsey's mansion called York Place. The King moved here from Westminster and re-named it Whitehall Palace.

Londoners were sorry to see the chantry chapels close down as well. This happened ten years later in Edward VI's time. One of the most famous was the chapel of St Thomas on London Bridge. Orders came that the chapel must close, but no one hurried to obey them. For years the chapel stood empty. Finally, it was turned into a grocer's shop.

Some of the monks' and nuns' buildings fell even lower than this. The nunnery of St Clare (called the Minoresses' Convent) became a warehouse for weapons and armour. All that remains is the name of a road parallel to Houndsditch, called the Minories.

Many other monasteries have disappeared like this, leaving only their names. Austin Friars, Crutched Friars, Whitefriars, Carmelite Street, Carthusian Street; which is the odd one out? The last one, since all the other buildings have disappeared, but the Charterhouse is still there. Spitalfields is all that reminds us of the Hospital of St Mary.

Westminster Abbey lost its monks but kept their buildings. Some are used today by Westminster School. Even St Paul's Cathedral did not escape altogether. When the Protector Somerset was building Somerset House, he pulled down St Paul's cloister to provide stone.

3
Elizabethan London

The Arrival of the New Queen

Today we remember each 5 November, but no one celebrates 17 November. Yet all through Elizabeth I's reign it was one of the red-letter days of the year. On 17 November 1558 news came that Queen Mary was dead and Elizabeth was queen in her place. She was young, pretty and clever, and Londoners looked forward to welcoming her to their city.

Every new king or queen made a coronation journey through London, and we know the exact route which Elizabeth took. With the help of the map made in 1575 (*see below*) you can follow her route and find out what she would have seen as she passed through London.

In this map (one of the very earliest we have) it looks as if each house is shown. In fact the map-maker has not counted the exact number of houses in every street: he just meant to give an idea of the different types of building in each part of the city. Only the more famous buildings are real portraits.

Braun and Hogenberg's map of London in 1575.

By now the City is beginning to expand over the line of the Roman wall. Ribbons of houses are spreading along the main roads out of London. London Bridge is still the only bridge. If you wanted to cross the river somewhere else you used a ferry, or hired a waterman.

Queen Elizabeth was staying in the royal palace at Hatfield when Mary died. At once she got ready to come to London, reaching it on 23 November. First she stayed for several days at the Charterhouse, and this is named on the map. It is drawn with three trees to show that it stands in a garden, just to the north of Smythefield.

Meanwhile Londoners were getting ready to welcome their new Queen. Two days later, on 25 November, she made her state entry through Cripplegate. This is the gate just to the right of the sharp angle in the wall, by St Giles' Church. The walls and gates were still kept in good repair, though the gates themselves were hardly ever shut now. St Giles Church, Cripplegate, is still there today.

Elizabeth then turned east along the road just inside the wall; she went as far as Bishopsgate, where the main road from the north comes into London. Then she went south-east towards the Tower, zigzagging along a route which included Mark Lane.

The Tower of London (spelt Towre) is very carefully drawn on the map. Elizabeth spent a week here; she must have remembered her visit four years earlier, as her sister Mary's prisoner. As well as this, she knew that her mother, Anne Boleyn, had been executed in the Tower. But in November 1558 everyone in the Tower wanted to make her forget the unhappy past.

The building where she stayed is at the south-east corner of the Tower. It was pulled down long ago, but the water gate she used is still there, and so are most of the buildings she will have seen.

The picture opposite shows the Queen's Lodging below and to the right of the White Tower and the water gate. This diagram was drawn at a time when the Tower still lay in open fields at the edge of the city. The great moat was filled with water; now it is dry and grass-lined. Thames Street, Tower Street and Barking Church (All Hallows Barking by the Tower) are still there. Find the scaffold on Tower Hill, where public executions took place till the nineteenth century.

Elizabeth went through the water gate to embark on the next stage of her journey, to Westminster. It was much quicker to go there by water than by road. The river was broad and straight, while the roads were narrow and twisting. So the Queen now sailed upstream in the Royal barge. She passed through the wide central arch of London Bridge, seeing the main buildings of the city to her right. St Paul's Cathedral stood out because it was the tallest of them all. It is not easy to see on the map, but it is the long building with a spire, immediately above the Royal barge.

Elizabeth landed next at Somerset House. She stayed here for a week because the royal palace at Whitehall was still not quite ready for her.

There is a Somerset House on the same site today, just east of the sharp bend in the river Thames. But the actual house Elizabeth stayed in was pulled down two hundred years ago. It is called Somerset Place on the map; Edward VI's Protector, the Duke of Somerset, had built it in the very latest French style in 1549.

Finally, Elizabeth had the short trip round the bend in the Thames to land at the royal pier in Westminster. You can pick out the jetty on the map, with a cluster of boats moored at it. Like every other monarch, she was to be crowned in Westminster Abbey, just south of Whitehall Palace. But instead of going straight to the Abbey on the day of the coronation, Elizabeth

The Royal Barge, enlarged from Braun and Hogenberg's map. The map-maker has used some odd spelling. Baynard's Castle is here spelt 'Benams Castle', while Paul's wharf is called 'Powle's warf'.

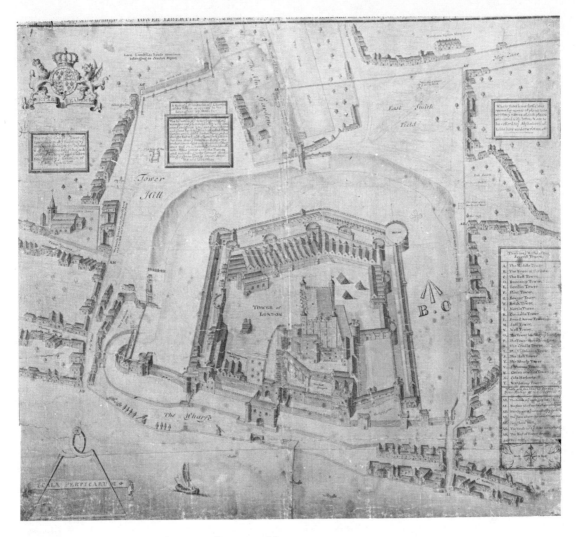

Plan of the Tower of London in 1597. Compare this with the photograph of the Tower today on page 22.

wanted to give as many Londoners as possible a chance to see the great procession.

So on 14 January she went back by river from Whitehall to the Tower. Next day she set off through the London streets in her coronation robes. Elizabeth wore a dress made of cloth of gold, and was carried in an open 'litter' with a canopy of gold brocade. A thousand men walked or rode at her side, dressed in crimson.

Wooden rails were placed along the route to hold back the crowds, but they were bright with coloured cloths. As there had been a light fall of snow that morning, everything was sparkling. People wore their smartest clothes as they waited for the Queen to pass. The members of the City companies looked best of all in their brilliant liveries, with furs to keep them warm.

The great procession stopped at several places along the route while specially written scenes were acted.

After leaving the Tower, the first stop was at Gracechurch (then called Grasse Church because of the hay market held there). Gracechurch Street is the broad road running north from London Bridge towards Bishopsgate. You can just make out a church tower on one of the street corners;

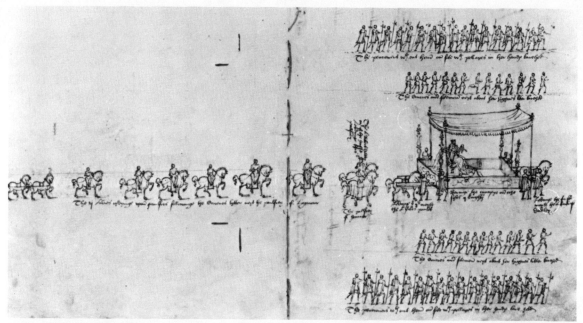

Part of Queen Elizabeth's coronation procession. This shows the Queen in her litter accompanied by soldiers, courtiers and musicians.

the church is no longer there, but there is a tiny alley called St Benet Place to remind us that the Grass Church was really named St Bennet's.

The second stop was in Cornhill by the water pump. Cornhill is the middle of the three streets which run east from the big church in the centre of the map. Next the procession stopped in Cheapside, the biggest shopping street in the city. Here the City Recorder presented the Queen with a purse full of gold, and she made him a speech. From Cheapside she passed beside St Paul's Cathedral, pausing while a boy from St Paul's School spoke some Latin verses (she was a very good Latin scholar herself, and certainly understood every word he spoke). Then she went down Ludgate Hill and out of the gate at the bottom. It was specially decorated for the occasion, and there was also music played as she passed through.

The final pageant was at Temple Bar, which marked the City boundary. You can see it on the map as a building right across the street, just to the north of the Temple. Today this is the place where Fleet Street changes its name to the Strand. Here at Temple Bar a choir of children sang to the Queen, and a boy dressed as a poet bade her farewell. They were rewarded by hearing her say 'Be ye well assured I will stand you good Queen'.

Now the procession wound its way westwards past Charing Cross and finally reached Westminster for the coronation. A blue carpet had been laid from the Abbey to Westminster Hall; here a vast banquet was held after the service. But the crowd disgraced itself at this point. The souvenir hunters were so keen to grab bits of this carpet that they tried to cut off pieces the very moment the Queen had passed by. The Duchess of Norfolk, walking behind the Queen, was in danger of being tripped up!

The coronation banquet in Westminster Hall lasted from three in the afternoon till well past midnight. After the meal itself there were masques and dancing, and the Queen's Champion rode into the hall in full armour. For ten days the festivities went on, though all must have been quiet again in the City long before they ended.

The Homes of Elizabethan Londoners

After the coronation Queen Elizabeth lived in Whitehall Palace. But she often went back to the City, and if she arrived on a public holiday, the visit soon turned into a carnival. The first time this happened was on St George's Day (23 April) 1559; everyone had a day off work for England's patron saint.

The Queen had sailed along the Thames from Whitehall to Baynard's Castle to have supper with the Earl of Pembroke. In the map it is just above the royal barge, but is spelt in a curious way: 'Benains Castle'. After they had finished their supper, the Queen and the Earl went out on the river in the Royal barge. Hundreds of small boats swarmed around them to give their owners a chance to greet the Queen and have a good look at her. One of them wrote later 'for the trumpets blew, drums beat, flutes played, guns were discharged, squibs hurled into the air as the Queen moved from place to place. And this continued until ten o'clock at night when the Queen departed home'.

Baynard's Castle was at the eastern end of a string of great houses beside the river. Somerset

The Royal Exchange. In the picture you can see a seat running along the back of the arcade, where the merchants could meet and do business. Today the rebuilt Royal Exchange is used for exhibitions and concerts, and the Stock Exchange is in Throgmorton Street.

House, where Elizabeth stayed before her coronation was one of them. Durham House, home of Sir Walter Raleigh, was another. By Elizabeth's time there were houses all along both sides of the Strand from the city to Westminster. Although there were still open fields beyond the houses, London and Westminster were joining up.

Most of the houses in the Strand belonged to courtiers or members of the government. Rich business men went on building homes in the City itself. One of these was Sir Thomas Gresham, who built himself a house in Bishopsgate. It was not such a fashionable place as the Strand, but his house was splendid enough for the Queen to visit him there.

Gresham invited her to dine with him, and then to open another new building of his in the City. This was the Exchange. Sir Thomas did a lot of business in Antwerp, where they had a large Merchants' Bourse or Exchange. So he made up his mind to build one like it in London.

Gresham was rich enough to pay for the whole building himself, but the city companies gave him the site in Cornhill. As the London merchants got used to doing business here, he hoped that London would become a great centre for traders from all over Europe.

Byrsa Londinensis vulgo the Royal Exchange.

Queen Elizabeth seems to have approved of the new building. We are told that 'She caused the same Bursse, by an herald and trumpet, to be proclaimed the Royal Exchange'.

Above the arches on the first floor Gresham provided room for shops. He wanted all sorts of different traders to rent shops here, as they do in a modern shopping centre. This was at a time when it was still unusual even to find a variety of shops in one street! The shops of one trade were mostly in the same street, as they had been in the middle ages. You still went to Poultry when you wanted a chicken, or to Ironmonger Row when you needed to buy a saucepan.

Only London's two main shopping streets, East and West Cheap, already had many different types of shop alongside each other. These roads were wide enough to have food stalls standing in the roadway itself; you can see them in the map, just above a church tower.

The shop fronts have not changed much since the middle ages. There are still shutters which let down by day to make a counter in front of the shop. The canopy was a new idea, protecting customers from the rain. You can see it behind and to the side of the stalls in Cheapside (the modern name for West Cheap).

Most of the Londoners shopping here went home to much smaller houses than Sir Thomas Gresham's or Lord North's. Many would be shopkeeper's wives, living above the family shop. Though more goods were coming in now from overseas, many things were still made in the workrooms behind the shops where they were sold.

Like the shops, London houses had not changed their basic shape since the middle ages. They were long and narrow, usually with a shop on the street front, and a workroom and kitchen behind. Below this were the cellars. The main living room was on the first floor, and still known as 'the hall'. Bedrooms came on the floor above. Some houses were as tall as five storeys, with attics at the top where the children and apprentices slept. There were no bathrooms, and no sitting rooms in the modern sense of the word. If you wanted to make your wooden bench or chair more comfortable, you simply laid a loose cushion on it.

Staple Inn, Holborn. This was originally an Inn for lawyers, providing them with rooms and a dining hall. Now it has been made into offices, with shops on the ground floor.

Almost all the sixteenth-century houses in London have disappeared; most were burnt down in the Great Fire. There are only two left, and neither is an ordinary family house. One is the Queen's House in the Tower of London. The other is Staple Inn in Holborn. Half of this was built in 1580, the rest a little later. Though there are modern shops on the ground floor with plate glass windows, the rooms above are Elizabethan. They give you an idea of the jutting-out bay windows and the pointed gables seen all over London in those days. The whole building is made of wood and plaster: first a timber frame was put up, then the walls were filled in with strips of wood with plaster between. If a Londoner wanted a bigger house than usual, he just built two of the basic houses beside each other, with doors opening between them. A really rich man might have five of these units side by side. At Staple Inn there are seven (though at one end a long upper window runs across the width of two gables).

You can see a later and even more decorated house front in the Victoria and Albert Museum. This was saved when Sir Paul Pinder's house in Bishopsgate was pulled down. Strictly speaking, a wooden front was illegal by the time this was built. Royal proclamations in James I's reign ordered brick and stone to be used instead of wood, to lessen the risk of fire. But few people took much notice, and Sir Paul built his house

The front of Sir Paul Pinder's House while it was still in Bishopsgate.

clear away or burn their rubbish. It seems that Londoners were not too keen on obeying; perhaps they were used to all the filth.

Yet they always had somewhere cleaner close at hand. Everyone in London had only to take a short walk to be out in open fields and away from the smells. Moorfields and Spitalfields really were fields, and close enough for an easy noonday or evening stroll. Even in the city itself there were trees and flowers; Hatton Garden and Covent Garden were real gardens then!

Entertainments

When a Londoner in the sixteenth century wanted to go to a show, he often took a boat across the Thames to the South Bank. Some people liked watching bear-baiting or cock-fighting in the wooden enclosures beside the river. For many others, a play was the best kind of entertainment. There were three theatres in the gardens by the river, close to the site of today's Bankside Power Station.

Early in Elizabeth's reign there had been no proper theatres. Plays had been acted on wooden stages put up in the yards of inns in the city. As more and better plays were written, men thought

Moorfields in 1559, from part of a lost map of London. The wall runs along the bottom of the map. Notice the clean clothes spread out to dry in Moor Field and the windmills.

(in 1611) in the latest fashion. Luckily the Great Fire did not reach as far north as this.

Perhaps these houses look quaint and cosy, but they were only slightly more comfortable than those of medieval times. Now that glass was cheap, everyone had it in their windows instead of canvas or horn. It came in tiny panes set in lead, which meant the windows let in less light than a modern one of the same size. The rich had large, decorated fireplaces now; poorer houses had an iron fireback in a recess at the side of the room. In both the smoke went out through a chimney instead of a hole in the roof.

There was still no running water or flush sanitation. No dustmen came round each week to collect household rubbish; the drains were open ditches down the middle of the roads. With the closing of the monasteries, St Antony's pigs no longer roamed about picking up scraps. The city council kept on issuing orders to the citizens to

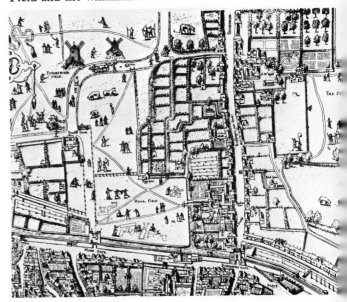

it worthwhile to build proper theatres for the first time. But unfortunately the Lord Mayor and the City Council disapproved of acting. Believing that plays encouraged people to behave badly, they would not allow any theatres in the City itself. The first theatres were therefore built just north of the city boundary in Finsbury Fields, and across the river in Southwark.

The earliest one of all, built in 1572, was simply called 'The Theatre'. Here you found a company of actors called The Lord Chamberlain's Men. Richard Burbage took the leading parts, and among the other actors was a man who also wrote plays—William Shakespeare. 'The Theatre' stood a little north of Holywell Lane (near Shoreditch High St). The audience walked there along Bishopsgate and across Finsbury Fields.

It was a round wooden building, with the stage and the central area open to the sky. Bad weather meant a small audience. Londoners knew when a play was going to be acted, because a flag flew above the theatre that day. A stage-hand blew a

Drawing of the Swan Theatre. This was one of the theatres on the south bank of the Thames. The stage juts out into the arena or 'pit', where people could stand to watch the play.

trumpet a few minutes before the play started to hurry people into their places.

No one bought tickets in advance. You paid your money to men at the door called 'gatherers', who put it straight into locked boxes (our term 'box office' comes from this). If you were young and poor, you could get in for one penny. This gave you the right to stand in the area in front of the stage, jostling elbow to elbow. For sixpence (or twopence in one theatre) you could get a seat in the galleries round the yard, paying an extra penny for a cushion. If you were keen to show off your clothes you might pay still more and get a seat on the stage itself. There was no curtain and very little scenery, as the stage jutted out into the yard.

Another difference from today was in the time the plays were performed. They started between two and three in the afternoon; there were no evening shows, and no intervals. If it began to get dark, torches were lit, but this was always dangerous in a wooden building. At least one wooden theatre was burnt down.

Behind the stage stood the 'tiring house' or dressing-room. The front of this provided a background for the actors, and also a balcony. When Shakespeare wrote a balcony scene in 'Romeo and Juliet', he knew the theatre had a ready-made balcony for it. All the costumes and props were kept in the tiring house. Elizabethan actors wore the clothes that were in fashion in their own day, even if the play was set in ancient Rome or medieval Scotland. No women ever acted, so the female parts were taken by boys.

In 1598, when 'The Theatre' was well established, the landlord who owned the site started to bully the actors. So Richard Burbage found a master carpenter to help him take down the entire building. By night the theatre was carried in pieces across London Bridge and rebuilt in Southwark. Here it was given a new name, the 'Globe'.

By that time there were five proper theatres in London, two to the north of the city and three in Southwark. The South Bank had become a real pleasure ground for Londoners. You took a boat at one of the piers upstream from London Bridge and asked the wherryman to row you to Paris Garden Stairs. We know what this cost around

1610 from 'Prices of Fares and Passages to be paid to Watermen' printed by the Queen's Printer, John Cawood. 'Item that no whyrymanne with a pare of ores take for his fare from Paules Wharfe, Quene hithe, Parishe Garden or the Blackfryers to Westminster or Whitehal or lyke distance to and fro above iij d'.

Paris Garden Stairs were to the west of London Bridge, about opposite Blackfriars. Here were the bull- and bear-baiting rings as well as the three theatres. Sometimes there was danger in watching the bears—one Sunday in 1583 the seats collapsed and eight people were killed.

Important foreign visitors might be taken to see the baiting. There was even an official called the Royal Bearward, who saw that his bears were well fed on butchers' throw-outs. The bears had names, of course. One favourite female bear was called 'Little Bess of Bromley', and the name of another was 'Hunks'. When the Duke of Wurtemberg in Germany paid a visit here 'His Highness was shown in London the English dogs, of which there were about a hundred and twenty, all kept in the same enclosure, but each in a separate kennel'.

But bear-baiting must have been losing favour by 1613, because that year the Beargarden was converted into another theatre, and named the 'Hope'. One of the first plays to be acted here was *Bartholomew Fair* by Ben Jonson. In this play one of the characters refers to 'sweeping up the broken apples for the bears within'.

Elizabethan audiences often ate while the plays were being acted. Sellers of hot pies and fruits did a good trade. Theatregoers also smoked, and shouted out what they thought of the play. When there was no interval, one can understand the smoking and eating; but it must have been hard for the actors to speak against chatting and calling out.

Gradually, the smarter members of the audience stopped going to the outdoor theatres. It grew to be fashionable to see plays at the indoor Blackfriars Theatre instead (converted from part of the old friary). Here there were seats for everyone, and it was lit by candlelight. Shakespeare's company, who became the King's Players when James I came to the throne, acted here in the winter and at the 'Globe' in the summer. Plays acted by students and schoolboys were popular too. Queen Elizabeth went to the Inns of Court to watch the law students act; boys from Westminster School put on Latin plays for her.

What kind of plays did these audiences enjoy? History plays were very popular. Elizabethans were very proud of being Englishmen, and were intensely interested in past kings and queens. They also enjoyed plays set in far away times or places. Anyone who had been to a secondary school had a good knowledge of Latin, and there were many plays about ancient Greece and Rome.

Playwrights knew how much their audiences enjoyed watching fights. If they decided to come to the theatre instead of the bear garden, they still saw plenty of violence. Murders, duels, poisonings, battles, suicides—all were expertly performed by Elizabethan actors. Though the audience did not have nearly so much scenery as we have today, they were good at using their imaginations to fill out the background. Often the play included speeches to help the audience do this. In *Henry V* Shakespeare tells the audience:

> Work, work your thoughts, and therein see a siege,
> Behold the ordnance on their carriages,
> With fatal mouths gaping on girded Harfleur.

There was also a less pleasant side to the South Bank of the Thames. Part of it still lay outside the City's control. This area, known as 'The Clink', was a favourite place for thieves and prostitutes.

There were no less than five prisons in Southwark at that time. One of them was actually called the Clink, and there is still a road named after it on the site. Another place well known for its criminals was Alsatia. This was the district between Fleet Street and the river, east of Whitefriars Street.

Sixteenth-century London was full of beggars, people who either could not or would not find a job. It was often hard to tell a man who really deserved help from a 'sturdy beggar' who chose to live off the kindness of rich citizens. These men, sometimes nicknamed Clapperdudgeons, gave themselves nasty sores by rubbing poison

Four Elizabethan Beggars. The beggars on the left may be real cripples, or just pretending.

He only found out that it was a trap after the trickster had gone.

London had plenty of people who were in real need of help, too. A law was passed to make every parish raise money to pay for the old, the sick and the orphans within it. Many rich merchants gave money to build almshouses for old people. Henry VIII handed over the royal palace of Bridewell to be a house where poor women could be given work. It overlooked the Thames near Blackfriars, and hundreds of similar workhouses were later named after it.

Sometimes all the members of a city company would join to help those in need. The Merchant Taylors' Company decided to start a free school for boys. Several of these schools founded by city companies still exist, though they have moved out of central London (Skinners, Merchant Taylors, Haberdashers, Stationers, etc.).

This meant that by the end of Elizabeth's reign London had a fair number of places for those in need. If you were sick, you went to St Thomas' Hospital in Southwark, or St Bartholomew's at Smithfield. If you went mad, your relatives put you in Bedlam (Bethlehem Hospital) where Liverpool Street Station now stands. Orphans were cared for by Christ's Hospital. Old people might go to several almshouses about the City, such as the one founded by Dick Whittington. For a medium-sized town this would have provided for everyone in need of help. But by now London had 200 000 inhabitants and it was not enough.

into cuts in their skin. Often false bandages and a limp were enough to coax money from a kind passer-by.

The most frightening beggars were the Abraham men who pretended to be mad. They only stopped bothering you if you gave them money. These rogues and many others came into the City by night to get a living.

Pickpockets were very common; so were cut-purses. These were known as 'Knights of the Horned Thumb', because they wore a horny sheath on one thumb, rather like a giant thimble. Elizabethan purses usually hung on cords from a belt. So the thief slid his horned thumb behind the strings, then cut against this sheath with a sharp knife. The victim felt nothing—until too late. Another specialist thief was the hooker; he put his long, hook-ended rod through open windows and fished fine linen sheets off people's beds!

Another well-known London trickster was the 'cony (rabbit) catcher'. Nicely-spoken young men would hang about the tombs in St Paul's to 'trap conies', or visitors from the country. The countryman would be offered a fantastic bargain or be told some tale of woe. One way or another he would be persuaded to hand over some money.

An Elizabethan wedding feast. The church on the right is St Mary's, Bermondsey. You can see the Tower of London in the distance on the left.

The Fall of the Earl of Essex and Elizabeth's Death

By 1600 there were other troubles besides the beggars and the sick. England was at war with Spain and Ireland was in revolt. The people of England, and above all of London, still loved the Queen. But some members of Parliament were getting critical. The Earl of Essex (once the Queen's favourite at Court) planned a rising which would force Elizabeth to hand over power to him.

Essex was in disgrace for having disobeyed the Queen, and he grew more and more mad with bitterness. He got the idea that he could win the support of a crowd of Londoners, if only he had the chance to speak to them. He knew that huge crowds gathered on Sundays to hear the outdoor sermons in St Paul's Churchyard. So one Sunday in February 1600 he set out to appeal to them. Two hundred supporters went with him from his house in the Strand. But they were too late. By the time Essex and his band reached St Paul's the sermon was over and the crowd had gone home.

Instead, Essex went to the Sheriff's house in Fenchurch Street. The sheriff was a friend of his, and might be persuaded to bring out the City Militia (part-time soldiers) to support Essex. But the sheriff would not help. He sent a messenger in secret to warn the Lord Mayor what Essex was up to. Essex started back towards Whitehall and found Ludgate barred against him. So he slipped down to the river and took a boat back to Essex House in the Strand. Alas, it was surrounded by soldiers loyal to the Queen, and Essex was arrested.

Elizabeth never forgave him. Seventeen days afterwards he and some of his followers were executed for treason. Three years later the Queen herself realised that she was dying. Whitehall was a cheerless place if you were old and ill. So Elizabeth moved to her palace at Richmond in January 1603. She had always called this her 'Warm winter nest', and here she died on 24 March.

The coffin was brought back by boat along the Thames for her funeral in Westminster Abbey. John Stow watched the procession go along Whitehall. The crowds of Londoners lining the route were 'sighing, groaning and weeping' at the loss of their beloved Queen. Stow believed that no other ruler had ever been so loved, and so deeply mourned.

Memorial to John Stow in the church of St Andrew Undershaft. John Stow published his 'Survey of London' in 1599, giving a detailed street-by-street description of London as he knew it. A memorial service is held each year in this church, at which a fresh goose quill is placed in his hand.

Questions on Elizabethan London

1 Compare the maps on p. 20 and p. 37 (Medieval and Elizabethan London). In which directions has London expanded furthest, and why?
2 Draw a sketch map to show Elizabeth's coronation journey through London. Underneath write a brief description of what she would have seen on the way.
3 Make a list of the warnings you might give to a foreigner coming to visit London in the sixteenth century.
4 Draw London Bridge in 1600. How does it differ from London Bridge today?
5 Think of the name of a play you could have gone to see in Elizabethan London. Then write an account of a visit to the theatre to see it.
6 Make a list of all the streets going down to the Thames from the Strand. Find out which of them are named after a great family which once owned a house there.

4
Stuart London

London in 1603 would look very small and crowded to us. But to James I, England's new King, it seemed a huge and rich city. He had only known Edinburgh before; now he had come to live in a city which spread for miles. London stretched from beyond the Tower in the east, all along the north bank of the Thames, almost as far as the Horse Ferry at Westminster. One building stood out from among all the others: old St Paul's Cathedral, with its short tower, where the spire had once been.

It was still much quicker to get from one end of London to the other by boat. The city streets were more crowded than ever. As the population grew, people added extra storeys to the top of their homes and sold their back yards for building. There were new houses outside the city, mainly to the east and west. But many Londoners preferred to live in the centre, in spite of the packed and dirty streets.

The City of London, drawn by C. J. Visscher in 1616. Notice all the landmarks along this panorama of London, from the bridge to Charing Cross. Old St Paul's is the biggest building; it must have been even more striking before it lost its spire (burnt by lightning in 1561).

A short way south of Whitehall lay the old Palace of Westminster. No kings ever stayed here now; it was too draughty and uncomfortable. All the rooms were used by Parliament and the king's ministers.

Coming from Whitehall, you first reached New Palace Yard. Westminster Stairs were on your left, the pier where boat passengers could land.

Westminster Hall was next, with St Margaret's Church just across the road. But both buildings were partly hidden behind houses and inns. St Stephen's Chapel, where the House of Commons had been meeting since 1547, was tucked in behind Westminster Hall. The House of Lords stood at right-angles to it. Only Henry VII's Chapel at the east end of Westminster Abbey stuck right out into the road. All the other important places were buried behind private buildings.

In 1605 this helped to give the idea for a plot to a group of dangerous men. They were Roman Catholics, and they hated James for refusing to allow them to build their own churches or hold important jobs. Among them there was a group

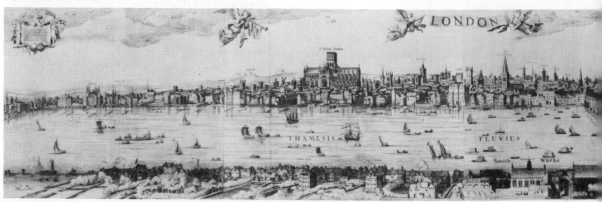

New Palace Yard, Westminster, drawn by Wenceslas Hollar. The artist stood with his back to the river. Westminster Hall is on the left, and the Abbey appears over the roof tops just to the right of it. The entrance to Whitehall is hidden among the houses on the right.

of extremists who wanted to kill James and all his government.

Robert Catesby was really their leader, though the man whose name everyone remembers is Guy Fawkes. The plotters rented a house next to the House of Lords (where the state opening of Parliament takes place). By boring a hole in its cellar wall they gave themselves a secret entrance to the vaults beneath the Palace of Westminster. The wall was very thick and the tunnellers were soon in despair. But then they were lucky enough to be able to rent the very vaults they wanted to reach! There was a back door to these vaults beside the river. Here Fawkes arranged for barrels of gunpowder to be delivered by boat under cover of darkness. By 5 November the plotters had packed in enough explosive to blow up the whole place. The King and his ministers, the MPs and all the chief men in the country would be there for the state opening of Parliament on 6 November—and they would all be killed.

But the plotters were betrayed to the government. Soldiers searched the cellars of the Palace of Westminster on 5 November and caught Guy Fawkes preparing a fuse. Catesby, Fawkes and several others were tried for treason and executed. To this day, the vaults beneath the Houses of Parliament are always searched on the eve of the State Opening of Parliament.

James also had pleasanter things to occupy him. Both the King and the Queen were very fond of watching plays and pageants, and even acting in them. Special shows were arranged for the Court to watch, called 'masques'. James asked the best poets to write the words for these masques and he found a brilliant young artist called Inigo Jones to design the scenery and costumes.

The execution of Guy Fawkes and his fellow plotters. Traitors were given a terrible death: to be hung, drawn and quartered. A large crowd gathered on Tower Hill to watch.

Portrait of Inigo Jones.

Inigo Jones was brought up in London (though his unusual name is Welsh). As a young man he had the chance to visit Italy. He came home with his sketch-books full of drawings of the buildings he had seen; the latest Italian palaces and the ruins of Ancient Rome. There are many ideas from Italy in the wonderful stage sets he designed for the King's masques.

Before long James started looking for a Court Architect. He wanted to add new wings to his palaces to make them grander and more up-to-date. James liked the building designs in Inigo Jones' stage sets, and found that he had original and exciting ideas for real buildings as well.

Inigo Jones accepted the job of Court Architect. He started by designing a house for Queen Anne at Greenwich which is still called the Queen's House. Like his stage sets, it is based on

The Banqueting House, Whitehall. It was built in 1619–22. Inigo Jones copied the classical pillars, the window designs and the balustrade from palaces he had seen in Italy.

the buildings he had seen in Italy. Many people in Europe were already copying this style, but Jones was the first architect to do so in England.

Inigo Jones' next work for the King was in Whitehall itself: a grand dining hall which could also be used as a theatre. The great Flemish painter Rubens painted a picture on the ceiling, but the thousands of candles needed to light up the actors and scenery gave off a thick smoke, and the beautiful ceiling soon began to turn black. Banquets could still be held in the hall, but a wooden theatre was built close by for the masques.

James allowed Inigo Jones to work for other people as well. The Earl of Bedford used him when he needed an architect to help develop his land north of the Strand. The whole area between Westminster and the City was filling up as London's population grew, so the Earl hoped to cash in on the demand for new homes.

The Earl's group of houses round four sides of an open space was the very first of London's many squares. It was called Covent Garden Piazza (using the Italian word for 'place'). Today there is nothing left of it except the church, St Paul's, Covent Garden.

All these new houses needed a good supply of water. There was a water wheel at one end of London Bridge, but it did not draw up enough water for all the extra homes. In any case, Thames water was not very clean for drinking.

Sir Hugh Myddelton had the idea of digging a channel to bring pure water from springs in Hertfordshire to London. In 1613 water started to flow along this 'New River' to a round pool in Clerkenwell. The water was then taken on into London through hollowed elm tree trunks. Finally it ran through lead pipes to each separate house which paid to be supplied.

After James died, Inigo Jones drew a design for a vast palace to replace the jumble of buildings at Whitehall. But it was too late. His new master, Charles I, had quarrelled with Parliament and he had no money to spare. In the end the quarrel grew so serious that the two sides went to war. Once fighting started the King had even less work for Inigo Jones to do. The architect actually got caught in the fighting himself. He was taken prisoner at the siege of Basing House in Hampshire, where 'the famous Surveyor Innico Jones was carried away in a blanket, having lost his clothes'.

Charles I had left London when he saw that the Civil War was about to begin. Most Londoners supported Parliament. A great many were Puritans who hated the King's kind of religion. Charles gathered troops in the Midlands and planned to march with them to capture London. London was by far the richest city in England; without its money, he could never afford to pay for enough soldiers and weapons to win the war.

The King had his first battle with Parliament's army at Edgehill. When news of it reached London, the citizens were terrified that their

Covent Garden Piazza. In the centre is St Paul's Church, which is still there. In front of it is the open area which later became a market. Later still, the market became famous for its flowers, fruit and vegetables.

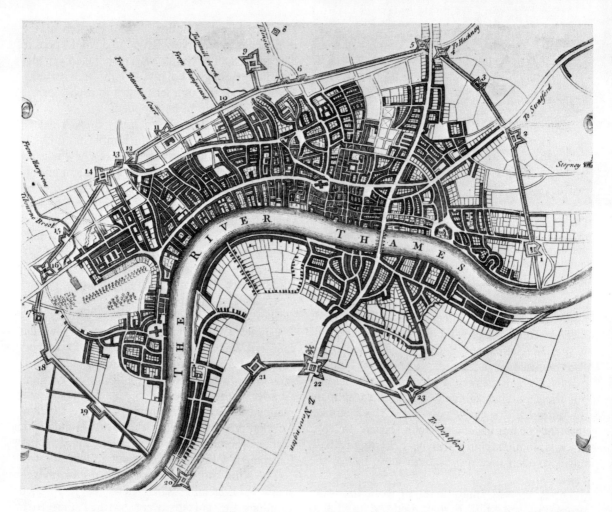

London in 1642–3, showing the defences against a royalist attack. You can see how far London has now spread beyond the old walls. Follow the earthworks round to number 15. Mount Street, Mayfair stands here now.

homes would be attacked next. They set up posts and chains across the main streets and offered to build an earth bank round the city.

As Charles and his army approached London, the citizen-soldiers known as the 'trained bands' marched out to stop them. At first the royal troops drove them back. Then at Turnham Green (near Chiswick) the tide turned. The King's soldiers were tired after their long march south. They saw that the Londoners were well dug in with trenches and guns, and getting new recruits every day. Charles decided it would be wiser to turn back. He would attack again next spring.

The people of London made sure the King would have a hard fight when he tried to capture their city. As the evenings lengthened in the spring, people went out after work with spades to complete the defences. The nave of St Paul's Cathedral was turned into a cavalry barracks with 800 horses in makeshift stalls.

People grew more and more anxious as they waited for the attack. To make them gloomier still, the Londoners were allowed no plays or bear-baiting. Even the Lord Mayor's Show was stopped to save money for the defence of the city.

In fact the King and his army never came anywhere near London again. Parliament's army was far too strong for them, and won all the main battles of the war. Finally Charles I was taken prisoner. When he escaped and began fighting again, Parliament decided he could no longer

The King faced them, sitting on a red velvet chair. There was a partition behind Charles, and the general public were allowed beyond it. All they could see of the King was his black hat.

During the week of the trial, 20–27 January, the King slept at Sir Robert Cotton's house in the heart of the Palace of Westminster. Charles was found guilty of treason for waging war against his subjects, and sentenced to death. For his last few days of life he was moved across to St James's Palace. Here his two younger children (Elizabeth, aged thirteen, and the Duke of Gloucester, aged eight) came to see him for the last time. His older children were in exile in Holland with the Queen.

Charles' execution was fixed for 30 January. A special platform was built for it in front of the Banqueting Hall in Whitehall. Cromwell chose this place because only a small crowd could fit into the area beside the platform. He feared a riot if the King was beheaded in a great open space such as Tower Hill.

In fact the weather was so bitterly cold that no one wanted to stand about for long. Even the Thames was frozen, and snow had begun to fall.

Charles walked across St James's Park on the morning of 30 January, wearing an extra shirt to stop himself shivering. He climbed a staircase into Whitehall Palace, along a gallery hung with the

Charles I's trial in Westminster Hall. This is the inside of the hall shown on page 49. The King is sitting in the centre with his back to the public. Find the Lord President and the Commissioners in their tiers of seats.

have any power. The leader of the army, Oliver Cromwell, wanted an even more drastic end for him: trial and death.

Charles was brought to London on 19 January 1649. No ordinary court of law had the right to try the King; special judges and a suitable hall had to be found.

Cromwell chose Westminster Hall for the trial. Here there was plenty of room for the public to come and watch, though carpenters had to work quickly to put up seats and barriers. They built tiers of seats at one end for the 130 special judges.

The execution of Charles I in Whitehall, January 1649. This picture was very popular at the time, but some of the details are wrong. You can find a few by comparing it with the picture on page 51.

paintings he had so enjoyed collecting. Then he crossed the street by the bridge and came into the Banqueting Hall.

The executioner was waiting on the platform as the King stepped out of one of the first floor windows. Charles took off his jewelled chain and his waistcoat. Then the crowd became completely silent as he laid his head on the block.

When the axe fell, a terrible sound of anguish came from the people watching. Later one boy who had been there remembered it as 'such a groan as I never heard before, and desire I may never hear again'.

England had no king; she was now a republic. Oliver Cromwell and his soldiers (nicknamed Roundheads) controlled the country. Parliament gave Hampton Court Palace to Cromwell as his official residence. But when he had business in London he slept at the Palace of Whitehall.

Cromwell and his supporters were strictly religious men. They banned duelling, swearing, cock-fighting and horse racing. The London theatres were closed for good, the cocks and the baiting bears were killed. Some Londoners disliked this severe rule. Others just hated the soldiers who always seemed to be about, searching houses and telling people what to do.

Few citizens were very sad when Oliver Cromwell fell ill in 1658. His doctors moved him from Hampton Court to Whitehall for a change of air. But it did no good, and he died shortly afterwards. The body lay in state in Somerset House, then it was privately buried in Henry VII's Chapel in Westminster Abbey. A public funeral was held a month later. The route of the mourners was lined with soldiers, all dressed in new red coats with black buttons.

Less than eighteen months later England had a King again. Cromwell's son was hopeless at running the country, and people were only too glad to welcome Charles II as their king. London streets were strewn with flowers and every church rang its bells as he entered the city on 29 May 1660.

This is the period known as the 'Restoration'. Many people came back from exile in company with the king. They were determined to have a gay time to make up for the lean years. Theatres re-opened and new ones were built. Actresses appeared in public for the first time; one of them

The house where the first plague victims died, at Ashlin's Place off Drury Lane. Ashlin's Place was in the parish of St Giles-in-the-Fields. There were strict rules against more than one family living in a house in the City. So areas like this, just outside the City boundary, had become terribly over-crowded.

54

was called Nell Gwynn. King Charles lived in Whitehall, while his brother James, Duke of York, was across the park at St James's Palace.

Londoners did not have many years of uninterrupted enjoyment. The plague (which had returned again and again in small outbreaks ever since the Black Death) hit London in a great attack in 1665.

London had not only gained streets of elegant new houses as the population grew. Her slums had also become bigger and dirtier. One of the worst was the area round St Giles-in-the-Fields, north of Charing Cross. Another was the district between Ludgate and Newgate. Here were many tanneries and slaughter houses, and butcher's offal was flung out into rubbish heaps. No wonder one street was called Stinking Lane.

It was in St Giles that the first people fell ill with plague in the winter of 1664–5. With the warm spring weather, the number of cases went up. The City Council made a rule that every house with a plague victim in it must have a red cross marked on its door. By early summer it was common to see houses with this sign.

Rich people left London to try to escape from the terrible disease. The diary writer Samuel Pepys, in his entry for 21 June, noticed the streets full of carts taking people away. Many shops were shut and homes were empty. Very few doctors stayed behind to care for the sick and dying.

As the number of dead continued to increase, it became a problem finding room to bury them. Carts were sent round each night to pick up the corpses, with a bell ringing to warn people they were coming. Special mass graves had to be dug when the churchyards were full. One was in Finsbury Fields, another was as far out as Highgate.

By mid-August the deaths had reached more than 5000 a week. Many cures were tried, but

Burying the victims of the Plague. The City churchyards were too full to take the thousands of plague victims. New burial grounds had to be opened in the fields outside.

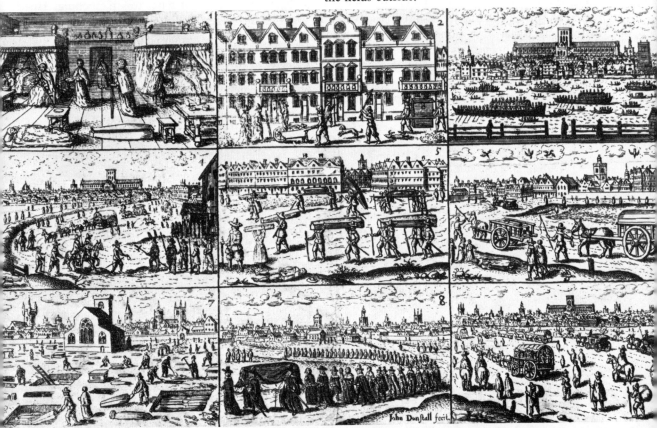

John Dunstall fecit.

55

none did any good: bonfires in the streets, strange mixtures to drink, poultices to put on the huge boils suffered by the plague victims, even killing all the dogs and cats in London. This last 'cure' did more harm than good. No one then realized that the plague was really spread by fleas which lived on rats. By killing the dogs, more rats stayed alive.

At last the plague died down as the weather grew cooler. The King and his courtiers returned to London and the shops began to open up. The official death total was 56 000. Yet many plague victims were never listed, so the real figure was probably much higher.

Hardly had London recovered from one blow when another struck. The crowded, dirty homes which helped the plague to spread could also be easily burnt.

London was always having bad fires. Most of London Bridge had been burnt down in 1633. But none were on the same scale as the Great Fire of September 1666.

On the evening of 1 September, the King's baker thought he had put out his fire in the bakery in Pudding Lane. Two hours later his son and daughter 'felt themselves almost choked with smoke'. Hurrying out of bed, they found the lower part of their house was filled with smoke and flames. They managed to escape through a top window. But soon the fire was so fierce that

the houses across the narrow street were also set alight.

A strong east wind fanned the blaze and sent the flames licking westwards. Here lay the warehouses by the side of the Thames. Barrels of brandy were stacked in some of them, tar and pitch in others; all these things caught fire easily. There had been no rain for weeks—everything was very dry.

By now everyone was awake. Along the Thames at Westminster a schoolboy was at morning service in the Abbey. In the middle of the sermon he noticed that people were moving about. News of the fire was spreading through the congregation, and the schoolboy slipped out of the Abbey. He was down by the river in time to see the first boatloads of refugees arriving from the City.

Samuel Pepys and his wife were woken by their maid at 3 am with news of the fire. But it had not looked serious from their house in Seething Lane, and they all went back to sleep again. Next morning Samuel climbed a turret in the Tower of London to find out what was happening. He saw the fire spreading along the river side and

London on fire, September 1666. A German artist's view of the fire, looking across from the south bank of the Thames. Samuel Pepys wrote: 'We saw the fire as only one entire arch of fire from this to the other side of the bridge and in a bow up the hill'.

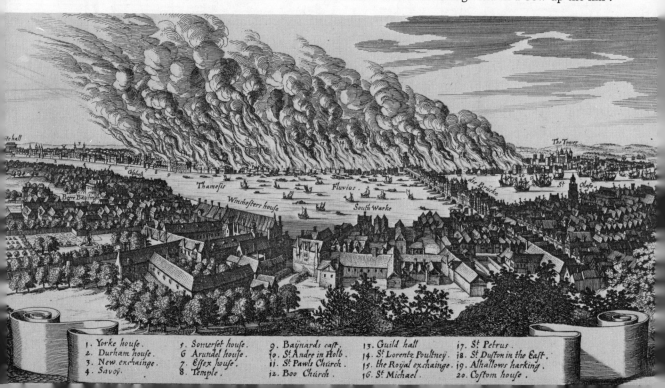

1. Yorke house.
2. Durham house.
3. New exchainge.
4. Savoy.
5. Somerset house.
6. Arundel house.
7. Essex house.
8. Temple.
9. Baynards cast.
10. St Andre in Holb.
11. St Pauls Church.
12. Boo Church.
13. Guild hall.
14. St Lorentz Poultney.
15. the Royal exchainge.
16. St Michael.
17. St Petrus.
18. St Dufton in the East.
19. Alhallows harking.
20. Coftom house.

went down to take a closer look. People were piling their goods onto boats and casting off into mid-stream for safety. In all the bustle he noticed how pigeons kept flying too near the flames and getting their wings singed.

The Lord Mayor should have been in charge of fire-fighting, but he was in a panic. So Pepys went to Whitehall, where he worked as a civil servant, to tell the King how little was being done to stop the fire spreading. Charles and his brother James came at once to see the fire for themselves. They ordered rows of houses to be pulled down to make fire-breaks.

Still the fire spread. By Monday night the whole river bank was alight as far as Baynard's Castle. It crept north to Cheapside, destroying many shops and churches.

By now a huge area was on fire. As far away as Oxford, the sun appeared blood-red through the layer of smoke. Fragments of charred paper were blown to Windsor.

At first it seemed that St Paul's Cathedral was going to escape. All day Tuesday, 4 September, it stood unharmed among a circle of burning buildings. The booksellers who had their shops all round the cathedral stacked their stock in the crypt for safety.

Unluckily the Cathedral was being repaired at this time, and so it was covered in wooden scaffolding. This caught alight on Tuesday evening. Next it set fire to the wooden roof. That in turn melted the lead roof covering it. Molten lead began to run down into cracks in the stone-work and out of the doors into the street. Pieces of stone exploded with the heat, falling off first in flakes, then in great lumps as the wind reached gale force.

At last on Wednesday, 5 September, the wind dropped. By now the soldiers were making large enough fire breaks. So even if the wind had gone on blowing, the fire would still have died down.

Everywhere lay heaps of smoking rubble. People picked their way among them, scorching the soles of their shoes. Many of the narrower streets were completely blocked. Here and there a few undamaged towers and spires helped you find your way.

Londoners began to add up how much had been burnt. Over 13 000 houses and eighty-nine parish churches had gone; 100 000 people were homeless. Besides St Paul's, hundreds of famous buildings had been lost. One that had escaped was the Tower. The east wind meant that the main damage lay to the west of Pudding Lane. It was just as well, as the Tower was full of weapons and gunpowder.

In the days that followed, people began to think how the City should be rebuilt. An office was set up in each City ward where people could hand in details of what they had lost. Today insurance companies would pay for rebuilding after a fire; at that date they did not exist. The huge cost was paid partly by private owners, partly by a tax on coal coming into London by sea.

At least four planners had drawn up new designs for the City within a week or so of the fire. They all wanted a new street lay-out, with broad, straight streets and plenty of open space.

But everyone wanted his new home to be exactly where the old one had been. No one was willing to move so that the new designs could be put into action. In the end the city was rebuilt almost exactly along the old, crowded, narrow street plan. A royal decree laid down that only brick or stone could be used. At least there would be no more wooden houses to catch alight so easily.

The City Council ordered a vast monument to be set up near Pudding Lane; Londoners would never be able to forget the fire. You can still climb up this great pillar and get a view over the City from the top.

Bricklayers, stonemasons and carpenters flocked into London from all over England. New brick-fields were dug in Moorfields and St Giles'. Sir Christopher Wren was given the mighty task of replacing St Paul's and forty-five of the burnt parish churches. No two churches that he built are alike: this meant he had to think of forty-five different designs. St Paul's was an even bigger problem. Londoners wanted a truly impressive building. If possible, it should have a dome or spire which could be seen for miles around. Wren made wooden models to help him decide on a design, changing them as new ideas came to him.

The houses and parish churches were rebuilt in a very few years. But St Paul's took far longer.

Wren was an old man by the time it was finished in 1709. As was fitting, he was buried in the cathedral. There is a simple Latin sentence on his tomb; in English it means 'If you seek my memorial, look round you'. He deserved it, because he gave London a cathedral as fine as any in the world.

Now that the City was rebuilt, work could start again on new houses elsewhere. The western edge of London became the most fashionable place to build a house. One of the smartest streets was Piccadilly; this odd name may come from a Dutch word 'pikedillekens', meaning a tip or corner of cloth. Piccadilly was once the tip of the built-up area of London. Some of the streets off Piccadilly are named after people who built houses here: Clarges St, Bond St, Sackville St and Burlington Arcade. Lord Berkeley built the square which is named after him.

To the south of Piccadilly lay St James's Palace and its park. Charles II loved to walk here from nearby Whitehall. He planted trees and shrubs, brought in deer and made a canal. Here, he could play his favourite game of pall-mall (pall-a-maglia in Italian, or ball-to-mallet). It was a cross between golf and croquet, and you needed a long alley to play it in.

There was already an alley just south of the main road from Charing Cross to Hyde Park Corner. Then players started complaining that dust from passing carriages spoilt their game; so Charles decided to move both the road and the alley. He re-routed the road along the Pall mall alley, and built a new alley south of the old road. The official name of the new road was Catherine St, named after Charles' wife. But Londoners always called it Pall Mall.

Meanwhile the Duke of St Albans had the idea of building on the empty land between Pall Mall and Piccadilly. He planned a large square of really grand houses, hoping that courtiers and nobles would buy them. He called this St James's Square, since the area had always been known as St James's Fields. The people who moved here needed a church, so the Duke asked Wren for a design. Today you enter this church from the north, not the south; it is called St James's, Piccadilly.

By 1700 there were houses in the roads leading off St James's Square and on both sides of Pall Mall. Those on the south side were specially splendid. Only one of them still stands, Schomberg House. There were elegant new houses to the north as well: Red Lion Square (north of the Strand) was started in 1686.

The plague and the fire were safely past; there was nothing to stop London spreading further and further.

A game of Pell Mell (or Pall Mall), showing one end of the long alley in which it was played.

Questions on Stuart London
1 How did the Civil War affect London?
2 Tell the story of Charles I's trial and execution, carefully describing the setting for both events.
3 Imagine how the plague might have hit one family living in London in 1665 and write a short story about it.
4 How would a serious fire be dealt with today?
5 Write a dialogue between two people arguing about the need for the tax on coal to pay for the rebuilding of the City churches.
6 Make a list of all the buildings in London designed by Sir Christopher Wren, and draw any one of them.

5
Georgian London

'And whither will this monstrous city extend?' wrote Daniel Defoe in 1724. Like all Londoners, he was amazed at the speed with which their city was growing.

In 1700 London consisted of the City, Westminster and a fringe of streets round this core. By 1800 all the outlying villages like Kensington, St Marylebone, Whitechapel and Stepney had been swallowed into the built-up area.

London attracted newcomers from all over Britain and even from distant countries. Young men and women came here to seek work at the rate of about 8000 each year. By 1801, when the first official census was held, there were 900 000 people living in London. London had become the biggest city in Europe.

As London grew, so did the contrast between its east and west ends. Mayfair became the most fashionable place to live. More and more rich people moved out of the City to find homes in the west end. Other rich people liked the quiet places which had recently been country villages, like Chelsea. Meanwhile the small, crowded streets to the east of the City were now lived in only by poorer people.

Anyone who owned land on the western edge of London could make a fortune very easily. When a land-owner (Sir Richard Grosvenor, for example) wished to develop his land, he usually sold it off in many separate plots. These were on leases for a set number of years; they also laid down strict rules about the shape of house to be built. Usually the houses had to be in straight rows, all of the same height. Often they were laid out on four sides of an open area. The result was the elegant squares which still survive in the West End: Grosvenor, Hanover, Cavendish and Berkeley Squares.

These houses were usually five floors high.

The kitchens were in the basement and the servants slept in the attic. The front door nearly always had a room with two windows beside it. The main reception room would be on the floor above. The houses in the grand squares were really large; these first floor rooms were huge enough to hold a ball in them.

Part of John Rocque's map of London, 1749. Tiburn Road, at the top of the map, is now Oxford Street. Tiburn Lane is now Park Lane. Many of the streets are the same today, though some spellings have changed.

A great many servants were needed to light the fires, clean and polish, cook and wait at table. Hardly anyone can afford to live in a house like this nowadays. Most of them have been rebuilt or converted into flats and offices.

Sir Richard Grosvenor and the other land-owners each wanted to make his new square into a real community. This meant building shops, a market, a public garden and perhaps a church. These would be in the side streets round the main square. Here, too, there were homes for the people who worked for the owners of the big houses.

At first the people living in and round Grosvenor Square had to walk through a wood to their nearest church—St George's (which was very handy for the people in Hanover Square). Then Sir Richard Grosvenor decided to build them a chapel much closer by. He called it the Grosvenor Chapel, and it is still there in South Audley Street.

St George's Church, Hanover Square. The lists of churchwardens, painted on panels inside the church, include several famous names. Hanover Square was a very fashionable place to live in the 18th Century.

The smaller roads round the main squares are often named after the same family (or its proper-ties). For example, Davies Street is called after Sir Richard Grosvenor's mother (Davies was her maiden name) while Audley was his grandfather's name.

Nearby, a man called Robert Harley, Earl of Oxford, married Lady Henrietta Cavendish Holles. The square they built is called Cavendish Square. Harley Street runs beside it, Henrietta Street runs west, Holles Street lies just to the south. Nearby there is Wimpole St, named after a village where the family owned land.

Sometimes the owner built himself an extra large house at one side of his square. Or he might sell the plot to another rich man to do the same. The Duke of Chandos never built the mansion he planned on the north side of Cavendish Square (because he died of grief when he lost his baby son), but Chandos Street is still close by. All through the eighteenth century rich noblemen were building themselves large houses in the Mayfair and St James's area. One of these was Buckingham House, bought later on by the royal family. Very few of these huge mansions are left. They took up too much space in a very expensive

district. Crewe House still stands in Curzon Street (and is now the head office of a large business). Lansdowne House is at the south-west corner of Berkeley Square and is used as a club.

Only a tiny fraction of Londoners lived in these fashionable squares and mansions (or the ones built a little earlier such as St James's, Soho and Bloomsbury Squares). Many middle-income people like doctors, lawyers and officials lived in the streets being built north of Oxford Street. Usually the houses here were in even rows, looking like smaller versions of the houses in the big squares. There were also plenty of medium-sized houses in the area between the City and the West End. Most of those which are left are now used as offices, but there is one which has not changed. This is Dr Johnson's House in Gough Square (off Fleet St). Dr Johnson was very poor when he first came to London as a young journalist. He lived in sets of furnished rooms, one after

Dr Johnson's House in Gough Square (off Fleet Street). The two windows on the top floor (left) are in the attic where the Dictionary was written. The third window is bricked up. You often see blocked windows like this in 18th century houses because the government put a tax on windows.

another. Then he had the idea of writing an English Dictionary. No one had ever done this in a thorough and scholarly way. So he rented the house in Gough Square and took down the partitions in the attic. This made a long, light room where his six assistants could work. The table where they wrote is no longer there, but a copy of the dictionary is laid out in the room.

Apart from this change in the attic, the house is just like a family home of 200 years ago. The rooms are small, and panelled in painted wood. Each one has a little iron fireplace and furniture made at that time. It is one of the few places in London where it is not too difficult to imagine you are back in the eighteenth century.

About the middle of the century a new road was built to run from Paddington in the west to Islington in the east. Now it is called first Marylebone, then Euston, then Pentonville Road. It opened up a whole new area for houses. Shortly after this there came a lull in the rush of new building, followed by a fresh spurt in the 1780s. Portland Place was built to link Oxford Street with the new road. Land west of Cavendish Square was laid out as Portman and Manchester Squares. Brunswick Square was built further east.

The four Adam brothers arrived from Scotland just at this time. Two of them, Robert and James, were brilliant architects. Their designs were so elegant and original that they were soon in demand. They spent much of their time on great country mansions (Kenwood, for example, when Highgate was right outside London). But they also developed one London site for themselves.

Robert Adam had visited the ruins of the great Roman palace at Split (now in Yugoslavia). This gave him the idea for a 'palace' beside the Thames. He and his brothers bought the lease of a stretch of the river bank south of the Strand. Here they built a terrace of very fine houses, forming one carefully balanced unit. Underneath there were warehouses with direct access to the river. Robert called the whole building the Adelphi. But this was no longer the most fashionable part of London. The houses sold very slowly. In the end Robert Adam ran a lottery with houses for prizes, and the tickets were snapped up at once.

The Adelphi, designed by Robert Adam. Adam called his terrace the Adelphi, which means brotherly love, to show that it was one unified whole. The front doors of the houses open onto the road which runs above the arches. It was demolished in 1935.

All this new building used millions of bricks, tiles and slates, and tons of timber. Bricks were usually made on the spot. In fact people living near building sites were always complaining about the dirt and smoke from the kilns. Sometimes the builder was in such a hurry that he added ash and rubbish to the clay. This made rotten bricks, and Londoners got used to the crash of jerry-built walls falling down!

The early eighteenth-century houses had tiled roofs. Then slate quarries opened in North Wales, and after that most houses had slate roofs. Wood came from the Baltic; there were timber yards all along the Thames where it was unloaded and stored. More wood was used than today because so many walls were covered with panelling, and,

of course, there were no steel girders, only wooden beams.

Most Londoners never owned their own houses. Instead, they lived in one or two rented rooms. In poorer districts many of the houses were divided up into lodgings. The owner and his family would often live on the ground floor. He let the floor above to a better-off family, at a rent of around 12p a week. The cheapest parts of the house were the cellar and the attic.

Single people could live still more cheaply by hiring a bed in a room shared with several others. These rooms would nearly always be let furnished. A list of furniture for a rented room in 1767 reads: 'A bedstead with brown wool hangings, bed and bolster, small table, two old cane chairs, curtains, old iron stove'.

It does not sound very cosy. To make matters worse, many of these rented rooms were used as workshops as well. A tailor, barber or clockmaker might have his work-table and tools in the same room as his bed (perhaps with his family tucked in as well). So he spent all his time in the same cramped and stuffy place.

The worst over-crowding was in the districts just outside the City boundary. Several laws had been passed to stop fresh building here, but still people kept pouring in. The owners built extra floors on top of the houses already there. Or they built in back yards and over alley ways. The poorest people moved in, there was no sanitation, and the result was terrible slums. Two of the worst were St Katharine's (just east of the Tower of London) and the area round St Giles-in-the-fields.

Rich people hardly ever came into poor districts. You might be robbed, and the smell and dirt were frightful. In fact most Londoners kept inside their own district for most of their lives. They lived within walking distance of their work; wives, staying at home, used only the local shops and markets. Poor people never went away on holiday nor to visit relations. Anyone from another district was considered a stranger.

Many districts had their special trade. Weavers lived together in Spitalfields, sailors and dock workers in Limehouse and Deptford, clockmakers in Clerkenwell. Even in the West End, certain streets were famous for one type of person. Many artists lived round Leicester

The Little Sanctuary, Westminster. Westminster Abbey Sanctuary had been a refuge for criminals in the Middle Ages. They went on living in the area long afterwards, turning it into one of London's worst slums. The street next to Little Sanctuary was called Thieving Lane.

Square; Arlington Street was a favourite place for politicians. There were also streets that were well-known as thieves' lairs; Little Sanctuary in Westminster was one of them.

In fact London was more like a collection of many separate villages than one great city. Only when proper public transport started in the next century do you get the different districts drawing together into one whole.

If you were able to go back into a London street 200 years ago, you would be shocked at the smell and the muck. Open drains still ran down the middle of the streets. Rubbish still lay about in piles, often shoulder-high. There were no pavements. After dark the only light came from the small lamps which citizens hung up by their doors on moonless nights.

Down by the river there were great stacks of sewage in 'laystalls', waiting to be collected by barge. Carts came round to each house to collect this 'night soil'; no one had flushing lavatories yet. If you were well-off you had your own earth closet. When it was full you hired a man to empty it.

Everyone grumbled about the muddy, uneven roads. But nothing was done about it till 1762, when the Speaker of the House of Commons nearly had an accident. His coach lurched so badly as he was travelling to Parliament that he nearly fell out. It clinched the case for the Westminster Paving Act. This gave the Westminster local officials the power to pave the main streets. Gutters were to be laid at each side of the road. The side of the roadway was covered with slabs of stone. Proper street lights appeared for the first time, and the houses were given numbers. All this was paid for by a special local tax, the rates.

Other districts followed Westminster's example. As one street after another became even and well-lit, only the thieves and pickpockets were sorry. From now on, street sweepers kept the rubbish under control. The open drains were closed over. The river Fleet, which had been more like a stinking open sewer than a river, was at last covered.

As the population grew, to the south of the Thames as well, it was urgent to build another

Part of the Fleet ditch before it was covered over.

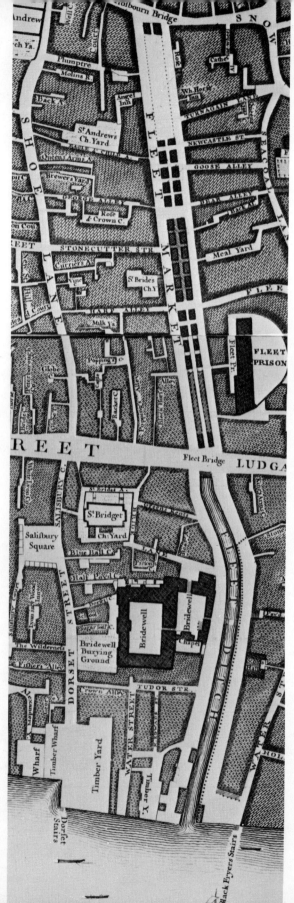

Section of Rocque's map, showing the River Fleet covered in. Londoners called the river the Fleet Ditch, because it was so filthy. Finally the City authorities decided to cover part of it over in 1733. This provided room for the new Fleet Market, in the centre of the map. Farringdon Street runs along here today.

Westminster Bridge, built 1738–50. The new bridge put the Horse Ferry out of business (though there is still a road named after it). Look for Westminster Abbey, Westminster Hall, and the four towers of St John's, Smith Square.

bridge. Work started in 1738 on Westminster Bridge, and in 1770 on Blackfriars Bridge. Neither of these had houses on them like London Bridge. People now realized these were just a nuisance, and a lot of them were pulled down.

If you were very rich, you went about London in your sedan chair (or you could hire one for an hour or two). Great nobles had running footmen to go in front of their sedan chairs, holding flaming torches.

Entertainments

If you lived in one over-crowded room, you were hardly likely to invite your friends round for supper. Instead, men liked to meet in public houses, often going there for the whole of every evening.

Even men with comfortable homes preferred to go out at night at this time. They went off to their clubs and coffee houses, leaving their wives behind to gossip and play cards.

Dr Johnson started a club which met each Monday night at the Turk's Head Inn in Gerrard Street. It started with twelve members, later rising to forty. His favourite place for supper on the other days was the Mitre Tavern in Fleet

A London Coffee House.

Street. Johnson also went to several coffee houses. At their height, there were 3000 coffee houses in London. Here you would have the chance to join in lively conversation, and to read the newspapers. The poet Dryden always went to Will's coffee house. He sat in the same chair beside the fire in winter, and beside the window in summer. Each coffee house had its special character. Some were great places for talk about politics. If you were a Whig, you would not dream of going to Ozinda's; if you belonged to the Tory party, you would be brave to go to St James's. Tories were, however, plentiful at the Cocoa Tree (as the name implies, this was a chocolate house rather than a coffee house).

Rich men also liked to go to their clubs; if you did not need to earn a living you could spend all day there. Some of these clubs had very fine buildings. Boodles, in St James's Street, was designed by a follower of Robert Adam. This club, and other famous ones like Brooks' and White's, were for gambling as well as for meeting friends.

Boodle's Club in St James's Street. The architect followed Robert Adam's style when he designed Boodles' in 1775. The members still play cards behind the big window on the first floor.

The Rotunda in Ranelagh Gardens. This is one of the London scenes painted by the Italian artist Canaletto on a visit. The word Rotunda simply means a round building. The concert platform in the middle is also part of a giant pillar to hold up the roof.

Pleasure Gardens

When the evenings grew light in the summer, at last there was a chance for all the family to go out together to enjoy themselves. If you set off on foot from central London you were in open fields within half an hour. Clerkenwell, Islington, Lambeth and St Marylebone were still in the country.

Tea houses and pleasure gardens were opening all round the outskirts of London in the eighteenth century. Here families could go on weekday evenings, or for the day on Sundays. After their walk from the centre, most families liked to rest and have a drink. They sat among the flower beds and enjoyed the fresh air and country views.

At Hornsey you could go for a walk in the wood beside the tea garden. At White Conduit House the owner kept bats and balls for his clients to play cricket. Hampstead had a well with healing waters as an extra attraction, and there was a ballroom for dances too. Several other gardens had mineral springs; Bagnigge Wells, Sadlers Wells, St Pancras Wells, for example. At the Peerless Pool near Old Street you could swim in one pool and fish in the other (and drink tea as well).

There was another kind of pleasure garden, mostly visited by people who came by carriage. Here the rich and fashionable Londoners came on fine summer evenings.

All these had first been opened just as public gardens to walk in. Then gangs of rowdy youths started making some of the popular gardens unpleasant for other people. So one by one the owners began to make an entry charge. Next they decided to provide something extra in return for this money. Concerts were arranged and people began to come in the evening rather than the afternoon.

Marylebone Gardens started charging for entry in 1737. The owner built a great room for balls and suppers, and hired his own orchestra and singers. A later owner wanted to make the gardens famous for good food. People could eat supper now as well as listening to music. Or you might buy his daughters' specially rich fruit cake to take home with you.

Later still, firework shows were started. But before long the public began to get bored. The gardens closed in 1776 and Devonshire Place and Upper Wimpole Street were built on the site.

At Ranelagh Gardens (next door to Chelsea Hospital) more was charged for admission since it was thought to be more select than Marylebone. This was a good place to go in rainy weather as well as fine. You could walk round and round the giant Rotunda, 555 feet in circumference.

In the centre of it stood a concert platform. Here the owners liked to ask well known people to perform. The eight-year-old Mozart played his own pieces on the organ and harpsichord when he was visiting London in 1764.

But the most famous Pleasure Garden of them all was Vauxhall. It lay south of the Thames, near the end of today's Vauxhall Bridge. In the early years people usually came here by river. Your boat tied up at the landing stage; then you walked down a dark, narrow passage. At the end of it you suddenly came out into the full blaze of lights.

Either you paid for a ticket at each visit, or you could buy a season ticket for the whole summer. Once inside you could reserve a box for supper. These were in rows all round the central area, open at one side like boxes at a theatre. Here you could eat Vauxhall's famous ham cut in paper thin slices. Or, like Lady Caroline Petersham in 1750, you could bring your own food. She stewed her minced chicken over a lamp with three pats of butter and a flagon of water.

There were several concerts each week during the summer. Usually these ended at eleven, and then the audience would enjoy themselves in the groves and tree-lined walks. On fine summer evenings the last visitors stayed on till the early hours of next morning.

A Frost Fair on the Thames. The river was wider and shallower than it is today. It often froze in the winter, and some years the ice was thick enough to bear coaches, stalls and even a fire to roast an ox.

Later in the century there were galas and balls as well. One of them, in masks, attracted 10 000 people. Later still, fireworks and stunt shows began. Madame Saquui climbed up a rope to a tower sixty feet high, then whizzed down in a shower of blue sparks. Hot air balloons, horse shows and carnivals drew in the crowds. But neighbours began to complain at so much noise late at night. The gardens finally closed in 1859. A church and several streets of houses went up on the site. Almost nothing is left of the London pleasure gardens.

Theatres and Concerts

At the beginning of the eighteenth century only rich people went to the theatre. Slowly the habit of theatre-going spread, and several new theatres were opened. The Theatre Royal, Drury Lane, was the most popular. Its manager, John Rich, made a fortune from a musical play called *The Beggars' Opera*. Soon he had enough money to open a second theatre, at Covent Garden. The great actor, David Garrick, used to divide his time between these two theatres. There was another Theatre Royal in Haymarket.

Theatre audiences were much worse behaved than today. If they disliked the play, they not only hissed and booed, but sometimes jumped up on the stage! One theatre put a row of spikes along the front of the stage to stop this.

An Opera House was opened in Haymarket, and also several halls for concerts. The strangest of these was Mr Britton's barn in Clerkenwell. Britton was a coal merchant by trade, carrying sacks to his clients on his own back. But he was also a great music lover and a friend of many fine musicians. He invited them to play in his converted barn. The smartest and the poorest music-lovers in London all came here to hear Britton's concerts; and there was no charge.

Prisons

Criminals had everything made easy for them in early eighteenth-century London: unlit streets, plenty of dark alleyways, almost no police. If you did get caught, many parish constables and even magistrates would let you go if you bribed them. Highwaymen grew so bold that they held up coaches in places as central as High Holborn. Thieves even stole the Great Seal of England from the Lord Chancellor's house in Great Ormond Street, and melted it down for silver!

But if you did get caught, you faced prison and very probably a death sentence. Central London had fourteen prisons at this time. Newgate was the most famous, lying next door to the Old Bailey where most of the big trials were held.

If you were rich, prison was much less of a punishment than it is today. Your friends could visit you whenever they wanted to. You could take in your own furniture and pay for good meals to be brought to you. Beer was actually on sale within the prison. But the poor suffered terribly. They were herded like cattle into overcrowded rooms. They were only given straw to sleep on. Unless they could bribe the gaoler, all they had to eat was a small loaf each day. Prisoners wore the same rags night and day all the year until they dropped off.

In the eighteenth century you could be put in prison for failing to pay your debts. Whole families went to prison and often stayed there many years. In fact most of London's prisons were for debtors. The Marshalsea, the Clink and the Fleet were three of the best known (hence our phrase 'in the clink').

Life was worst for the prisoners in some of the smaller gaols. At one of these, the Borough Compter, twenty prisoners had to sleep on their sides in a space 20 × 6 feet. The gaoler said that when he opened the door each morning the stench 'was enough to turn the stomach of a horse'.

There was little chance of escape. Any show of trouble, and a prisoner was put into iron fetters. The chaplain of Newgate wrote how he visited a man called John Bennett in 1730. He found the prisoner's legs so swollen by the extreme cold and by the irons on his ankles that he could not move them. Two days later he was dead.

Another serious hazard was gaol fever (typhus). The filthy, crowded rooms were breeding grounds for disease. If a man was sentenced to be shipped to the other side of the world—'transportation'—he might well die on the voyage.

Finally, for many prisoners the end came by hanging. After the trial they were put in the condemned cells (there were fifteen of these at Newgate). Each was 9 × 6 feet (3 × 2 metres) with one small window and a nail-studded door four inches thick.

Public hangings took place eight times a year at the Tyburn gallows (near Marble Arch). They were always on a Monday, and then everyone had the day off work. The procession through the streets from Newgate to Tyburn took half an hour. All along the route people gathered to stare. They watched the carts go past, each with a prisoner sitting beside his own coffin. The rope was already looped round each neck. At Tyburn itself the crowd was vast. Those who could afford it bought a seat in one of the special stands; the others just craned their necks and stood on tip-toe.

Hangings were one of London's most popular free shows. But, increasingly, some people protested, and in 1784 the processions to Tyburn stopped. After that the prisoners were hanged just outside Newgate itself. Yet even here the

Newgate Prison in 1792. The medieval prison in the gatehouse at Newgate has been extended many times. This huge new building was put up from 1768–78, burnt by rioters in 1780, and rebuilt. Now the Central Criminal Court (The Old Bailey) covers the site. The cattle passing in this picture are on their way to the nearby market at Smithfield.

A public hanging at Tyburn. Notice the specially-built grand stand on the left. Today there is a small cross let into one of the pedestrian islands at Marble Arch to show where the gallows once stood.

public was keen to watch. People paid for a place at a window of the Magpie and Stump Inn opposite.

By that time more and more people had become sick of all the crime and the cruelty. Two men in particular did a great deal to improve things. These were two London magistrates, John and Henry Fielding (who were half-brothers), from whom one could always be sure of strict justice; yet they could be very kind as well. Often a boy would come to them charged with pick-pocketing or stealing from a market stall. Instead of sending him to Newgate, the Fieldings might send him to sea to train as a sailor. The Fieldings also started London's first proper policemen, the Bow Street Runners. Before this there had only been part-time parish constables, with no training at all. All this helped to make the streets of London safer.

Hospitals

Perhaps one expects thieves and murderers to be treated harshly. But surely sick people deserved something better? At the beginning of the eighteenth century there were only two hospitals in London, St Bartholomew's and St Thomas's. Most illnesses were still treated at home.

As the population grew, it became clear that more hospitals were needed. Doctors were also improving their methods and more diseases and

A ward at Guy's Hospital in 1726. When Thomas Guy saw that St Thomas' Hospital in Southwark was getting over-crowded, he started his own new hospital beside it. The beds in this ward look roomy, but there was little air when the curtains were drawn across.

wounds could now be cured with the right treatment. A whole group of new hospitals was opened in London. The Westminster Hospital started in 1719; Guy's in 1725 (founded by a bookseller called Thomas Guy who made a fortune out of the South Sea Bubble); St George's was built at Hyde Park Corner to take advantage of the fresh country air in 1733; the London Hospital opened in Whitechapel in 1740, the Middlesex in 1745.

Guy's Hospital was designed to take 435 patients. There were twelve wards, each divided into wooden cubicles. The original staff were two surgeons, two physicians, a chaplain, a matron, eleven nurses and a bed-bug catcher. Like the other hospitals, it was thought to be splendid at the time. But it was very different from a modern hospital. The nurses were not trained and the wards were dirty (the bed-bug catcher always had plenty of work). The staff were amazed when one London surgeon told his pupils to stop spitting on the floor!

There were new maternity hospitals as well. So many mothers died during child-birth (and a great many babies died at once) that Dr Smellie and others decided that something had to be done about it. The hospital that was later to be called after George II's wife, Queen Charlotte, was founded in 1752, and there were several others. But midwives and doctors still never bothered to wash their hands, and only a few babies were born in hospital.

If you were in need of treatment, but could manage to walk, you might go to one of the new Dispensaries. Here a doctor looked at you and gave you medicine if you needed it. All this was free—not on the National Health Service, but

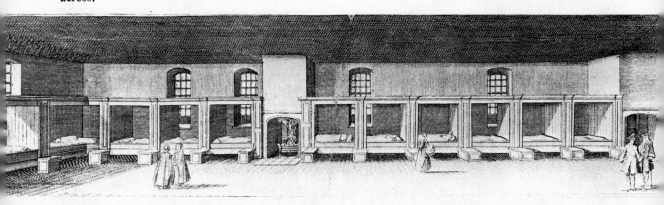

paid for by rich people who wanted to help the poor.

Mental illness was the last to get better attention. London had one huge mental hospital known as Bedlam. It had been rebuilt in a fine new mansion near Moorgate, but the patients were often treated cruelly. Difficult patients were chained up so that they could not move from their beds. The public even paid to come in and laugh at the lunatics; like the hangings, it was a favourite show. Doctors began to try new methods towards the end of the century. They realized that kind and gentle treatment did more good than cruelty, and the public were no longer allowed in.

Orphanages and Workhouses

If you were both old and sick you might end your life in a workhouse. Each parish had to provide for those who could not (or could no longer) earn their own living. In some places people were given money each week to keep them going in their own homes; but many parishes found it was cheaper to put everyone needing care into one building. They called this the Parish Workhouse.

Sometimes unmarried girls went to the workhouse to have their babies. Others were too ashamed to do this; they left the baby in a basket on the workhouse doorstep, or even out in the street. These were 'foundlings', orphans with no name till the workhouse matron gave them one. 'Tuesday Marrowbone' was found on a Tuesday in the parish of St Marylebone. You can guess where 'Friday Cripplegate' was picked up.

Once installed in the workhouse, the baby's troubles were still not at an end. Drunk and dirty nurses looked after them. Milk was a problem since proper feeding bottles and teats had not yet been invented. People suspected that many of the babies died, but no one could prove it.

Then an MP called Jonas Hanway decided to investigate. He went round every workhouse in London and asked the master how many babies and children were in his care. Then he asked how many had died in the past year. Finally, he was in a position to draw up a terrible list of figures. It showed that more than half the babies taken in care had died before they were one year old. In the worst parishes the figure was over 80%.

Hanway found that one parish (St James's, Piccadilly) sent its orphans to foster mothers outside London. Here the death rate was much lower. So Hanway was determined to make every parish do this also. He asked Parliament to pass an Act in 1757; after this all parish orphans had to be sent away from central London till they were at least twelve months old.

But what would happen to the orphans as they grew up? Most of them were sent as apprentices to learn a trade with a craftsman. Many girls became servants. No one took the trouble to see that they were well looked after. Mrs Meteyard and her daughters were unusually cruel; in the end they were executed for murdering their apprentice. They kept four girls in a tiny room making hairnets and mittens to sell in their shop in Bruton Street. The girl who died had been starved, then beaten.

Orphans for whom no master could be found were sent to work in cotton factories in the north of England (but not till the later part of the century).

As with Hanway and the babies, it was one specially determined man who tried to make life better for these children. Thomas Coram was a sea captain. When he was home in London between voyages, he was shocked to see newborn babies left on doorsteps. Sick children were also a common sight, left by their parents to die in the street. Coram decided to start a home for babies and children who had no one to look after them.

He had very little money himself. For several years he went round asking rich and powerful people to support his idea. Finally he had enough cash, so the government allowed him to get started. The foundation stone for a huge and splendid building was laid in 1742. Hundreds of people gave money to speed the work. One of them was the composer Handel, who conducted the 'Messiah' each year and gave the ticket money to Coram. Three years later the first children moved in. Their new home, the Foundling Hospital, must have seemed like a palace. Many of them had never had proper food, warm clothing, a bed of their own, or even a playground.

The Foundling Hospital. The site of the Foundling Hospital in Bloomsbury is still called Coram's Fields. The building was pulled down when the children were moved into the country in 1926. In this picture the children by the fountain are wearing the Hospital's special uniform.

Unfortunately people from far outside London now thought they could get rid of their sick children here. Soon it was over-full, and many of the children were already dying when they arrived. After six years the hospital had to close its doors. Afterwards it took only healthy babies and became an orphanage, rather than a hospital in the modern sense.

You can see that, by the later part of this century, very much more was being done to help the sick and needy. It was John Wesley who did most to stir the lazy consciences of the rich. Wesley was living in London when he had the experience which changed his life. In May 1738 he was at a service in a chapel in Aldersgate Street. Suddenly he had a vivid feeling that God was speaking to him; he felt he must go out to help the people no church bothered to try to reach. So he went to Kennington Common and a great crowd came to listen to his sermon in the open air. His friend Whitefield also preached out-of-doors; but at Moorfields he got pelted with stones and rotten eggs.

Later these men broke away from the Church of England and started their own Methodist Church. They needed proper chapels, and at first Wesley used an old iron foundry at Moorfields. Later, in 1778, he moved to a better building in the City Road. The Wesley Memorial Chapel is still there, with Wesley's own house next door to it. (The Whitefield Memorial Church is in Tottenham Court Road.)

By 1780, cruelty and violence seemed well on the decline. Then there was a terrible, brief return: the Gordon Riots. Up till this time, the treatment of people from other countries had been getting steadily better. Jews in Bethnal Green, French refugees in Spitalfields, Irish Catholics in Moorfields—they were all coming to be accepted as Londoners.

But in 1780 Lord George Gordon set up a Protestant Association. Its aim was to persuade Parliament to repeal an Act which made life easier for Roman Catholics. Lord George and his supporters drew up a petition and collected 44 000 signatures which they took along to the Houses of Parliament. They waited quietly outside all day, but the MPs refused to accept the petition. By evening the protesters were growing really angry. Lord George tried to cool them down, but they stormed off to attack several Catholic chapels close by.

They went home that night, but next evening they gathered beside a Catholic Chapel in Rope-makers' Alley, Moorfields. First the rioters tore down the chapel, then they damaged some Catholics' homes near it. By now there was a huge mob, many of them fighting drunk. When Mr Justice Hyde called out soldiers to break up the crowd, the rioters went and destroyed his house in revenge. Next they burnt down the house of Lord Mansfield (the Lord Chief Justice) in Bloomsbury Square.

By the third day the mob was totally out of control. They broke into Newgate, wrenching open the gates with crowbars. Then they released the prisoners and set the prison on fire. Next they attacked a whisky factory owned by a Catholic. Twelve thousand gallons of spirits stored in the cellars went up in flames.

Shops and homes owned by Catholics were looted and pulled down. Several other gaols were set alight and the prisoners set free. Finally, the rioters tried to storm the Bank of England. But by now 10 000 troops had been brought into London to stop them; the Bank held firm.

Hundreds of rioters were arrested and tried. Twenty-five were hanged, including Lord George Gordon. Dozens of buildings had been destroyed and 285 people had lost their lives.

Many of the rioters had been ordinary, decent men till that fatal week. Londoners were horrified to find what raging beasts a protest mob could become; and nothing on the scale of the Gordon Riots has ever happened since.

Trade

If a rich man wanted to buy a suit of clothes or some new chairs for his dining room, he came to London. Here he would find the biggest choice and the finest goods. So the shops provided not only for Londoners, but for people from other parts of England who came here to buy.

Shops had glass windows now instead of shutters. But until plate glass was invented the windows were divided up into small panes like the windows of a house. Fashionable shops sometimes had bow windows (there is still one shop like this in Haymarket—Freybourg and Treyer's). There were no ready-made clothes shops yet. Instead, you went to a shop to buy cloth, then asked your dress-maker or tailor to make it up for you. Shop windows showed beautiful silks and velvets, fine woollens and muslins. Shoe-makers and hat-makers displayed examples of their work to help you make your choice.

There were a great many barbers' shops. Some men went to one every day. The barber kept his clients' best wigs in special boxes and took them round to each house on Sundays before church.

There were still no really big shops. Each shop sold only its own goods, often made in a workshop

Trade card of John Flude, Pawnbroker and Silver-smith. Most shopkeepers advertised by giving away cards like this. Find the Pawnbrokers' three balls sign.

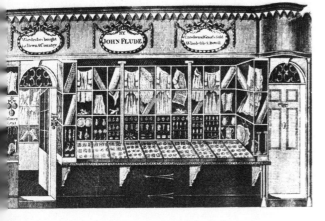

at the back. In central London most of the food was sold in markets, not shops. Each district had its own meat and fish market: Oxford Market was east of Oxford Circus. Shepherd Market is still the name of a small area in Mayfair, though the market has gone. If you had a really huge household to feed, you could go to Smithfield and buy a whole sheep or ox. The animal would have walked from the farm to London!

For some shopping you did not even have to go inside a shop. Street sellers went round calling their wares—'fine lavender', 'old clothes', all kinds of fruit in season such as 'cherry ripe'. Or you could buy hot fritters from a woman frying them at the street corner on a little brick brazier, calling out 'piping hot fritters'.

The real wealth of London came in by ship to the Port of London. By the eighteenth century ordinary people were beginning to buy goods from overseas. Before this, only luxuries, like silks and wine and spices, had been imported. Now everybody wanted sugar, tea, coffee, Indian cottons and eastern silks. In return, England sent out cloth, leather and metal goods.

The biggest and richest business in this trade was the East India Company. It had begun back in the time of Queen Elizabeth I; in 1726 it was doing well enough to build a huge new headquarters in Leadenhall Street. The other trading companies, African, Russian, Levant and Hudson's Bay, were wealthy too, and controlled most of the trade between England and their part of the world.

London was also developing as a centre for finance. By 1800 there were over seventy banks in the Lombard Street area. The biggest of all was the Bank of England. This moved into a large new building in Threadneedle Street in 1734. Insurance companies were also doing well and moving into bigger offices.

Today business deals still go on in the City, but the goods themselves are down the river in the docks and warehouses. In the eighteenth century they came into the City itself. The main docks for unloading goods from overseas were the 'Legal Quays'—five hundred yards of river frontage from London Bridge to the Tower, with an open area behind. In the middle of them stood the Custom House. Duty had to be paid at once

The Custom House in 1753. The Custom House in the middle of the 'Legal Quays'. Usually the Thames was far more crowded with shipping, with only a narrow passage left clear in mid-stream. By the end of the century the government had decided to build new docks further down the river.

on every cargo unloaded; as the quays grew more crowded, the queues at the customs desks grew longer and longer.

There were warehouses behind the quays. But many of the goods went straight off by cart to salerooms and stores further away. Some of the East India Company's goods were sold at an auction room in Lime Street. Here dealers and housewives elbowed each other to bid for fine silks and china.

If you look at a picture of London's riverside, you will see many smaller docks both above and below the bridge. Some of these had their special trade. Fish and coal were unloaded at Billingsgate, where the dock was set back from the river; flour came to Queenhithe (mainly from mills upstream); fruit to Three Cranes Wharf. The East India Company hired spare space at the Steelyard, once the great quay for steel bars from Germany.

The whole river below London Bridge was a forest of masts. Only a narrow channel was left free in the middle of the river to pass along. By the end of the century the over-crowding was

such that Parliament at last decided to order docks to be built further down the river.

Already the East India Company's ships were so big that they usually moored at Blackwall. Here their cargoes were unloaded into barges for the final journey into London. The company was rich enough to build its own ships, in a huge yard which was also at Blackwall. In fact there were busy shipyards all along the Thames shore below London. Timber yards appear on the maps too, since all the ships were made of wood. Ships need ropes, and Shadwell had a busy rope industry (there is still a Cable St there).

Besides the yards building trading ships there were the Royal Naval Dockyards. The main yard was some way down the river at Woolwich. Here warships were built in the deep water docks, then sent up to Deptford to be fitted with sails and rigging. Ship repairs went on as well. Even old sailors were provided for. Greenwich Hospital gave them a final home where they could watch the ships sail by and remember past voyages.

Along the river at Wapping, Rotherhithe, Poplar and Limehouse many sailors and ship builders had their homes. It is reckoned that a quarter of all Londoners in the eighteenth century got their living through ships and docks (and the dozens of jobs connected with them).

A view of Blackwall, looking towards Greenwich. Out in the river a group of East India Company ships are unloading their cargoes onto small boats (lighters) for the journey into London. A new East Indiaman is being built in the shipyard on the right. The twin towers of Greenwich Hospital show faintly in the distance, to the left.

Public Buildings

As the population grew, a great many more public buildings went up. There were fine new churches in Limehouse and Spitalfields as well as in the fashionable West End. The Mansion House was built for the Lord Mayor. Sir Joshua Reynolds started the Royal Academy and asked Sir William Chambers to provide it with a gallery when he rebuilt Somerset House.

Many of the new buildings were designed in the style known as 'Palladian'. Inigo Jones had brought the Italian architect's ideas to England in James I's reign, but they were too far ahead of their time and did not catch on. Lord Burlington discovered them afresh in the eighteenth century. He too went to Italy and sketched Palladio's villas. When he got home he put a new front onto his family home, Burlington House in Piccadilly. At Chiswick he built a villa which was a copy of one of Palladio's near Venice.

At about the same time Flitcroft designed the church of St Giles-in-the-Fields and William Kent designed the Horseguards in Whitehall which were also in the Palladian style: perfect balance or symmetry, and a portico as the central feature. In a simpler form it can be seen in all sorts of unlikely places—in a hospital (St George's, Hyde Park Corner), in a theatre (Drury Lane), in a bank (Bank of England). In the National Gallery and the British Museum it appears in a much grander form. Here it reminds you of the Greek and Roman temples from which the design came in the first place. This style continued to be used in the nineteenth century and well into the twentieth.

Questions on Georgian London

1 Draw sketch maps of Grosvenor and Cavendish Squares, and mark in the streets which were named after connections of the two families.
2 Describe an evening outing to Vauxhall Gardens.
3 Tell the story of a highwayman, from his arrest while holding up a coach to his execution at Tyburn.
4 What did Thomas Coram and Jonas Hanway do to help poor children in London?
5 A country girl comes to be a housemaid in a big house in Berkeley Square. Describe what her daily life would be like?
6 Make a list of buildings in London with a classical portico in front.

Regency London

When George III went mad, his son took over his powers and was given the title of Prince Regent. The Prince was very keen on building and town planning; he helped in the making of both Regent's Park and Regent Street.

Marylebone Park (the site of Regent's Park) had always belonged to the Crown. It had been let out on lease for many years, but this was due to expire in 1811. The man in charge of the royal properties (the Crown Surveyor) saw what a gold-mine lay here. Just south and east were the new estates developed by the Bedford and Portland families. Now it looked as if the royal family would have the chance to make some money the same way.

The Crown Surveyor invited plans to develop Marylebone Park. But no one seemed very interested. It was still some way out from the centre of London, with no good road leading to it. Then the Prince Regent was introduced to a young architect called John Nash. The Prince liked Nash's drawings. Soon he asked him to design projects for him in Brighton and London, and by 1810 the Prince had given Nash the job of designing the whole development of Marylebone Park.

Nash planned it as a park with houses for rich people all around it. Most of the houses were to be built in terraces, with grand decorations linking them together. Cumberland Terrace is the most splendid. It has a huge pediment on top and rows and rows of pillars along the front. Chester Terrace has a great arch. Hanover Terrace has domes at intervals along it.

The terraces all match each other in spite of these differences. This is because the basic style (classical) is the same throughout. So is the material used—cream painted stucco (plaster). Even the single villas set in the central parkland are in the same style and material. Nash did not invent a new design; but he was the first man to have the idea of placing terraces like this in a country setting.

He wanted to make a home for a whole community at Regent's Park. There were smaller houses for servants and shopkeepers set behind the main terraces. He also built three markets (one had a vast icehouse underneath, supplied by a ship sailing to Norway and back all the time). Later, one corner of the park was sold as a site for London Zoo.

Nash also planned a lake among the trees in the centre of the park, and he wanted a canal to run straight across from side to side. But the new owners did not like the idea of barges going close to their houses, so Nash altered the path of the canal so that it ran along the northern edge of the park. It linked up with the Grand Junction Canal over to the west (they join by Little Venice near Paddington). Eastwards, it ran for several miles before curving south to join the Thames at Limehouse. A canal was a money-making project at this time as it was the best means of carrying bulky and heavy goods before the invention of railways.

Oddly enough, the main house planned for Regent's Park was never built. This was to have been a summer villa for the Prince. Instead, he kept to his main London home, Carlton House (just beside the Mall). Nash and the Prince Regent had planned to build a road to join Carlton House to his summer villa. Even without the villa, the road was still needed. All the new inhabitants of the park would use it to get quickly into central London.

Nash's new road cut through the maze of small streets like a hot knife through butter. You can best follow its route on a map. It starts at Waterloo Place behind Carlton House Terrace, then runs north up Lower Regent Street to Piccadilly Circus. Then Regent Street itself curves gracefully north westwards before sweeping up to cross Oxford Street at another Circus. Next there is another bend to bring the road into line with Portland Place (which was there already) ending in Park Crescent and the way into the park across the New Road.

Nash insisted on designing the fronts for all the buildings in Regent Street. This was the only way to get them all to match. Some owners objected, and it was only the Prince's backing which kept the whole plan from collapse. Nash put an extra front along the curved part of Regent Street. This was known as the Quadrant. It looked extremely elegant, but the shopkeepers did not like it. So it was pulled down in 1848.

Nash's last job for the Prince was to enlarge Buckingham House. George III's wife had moved there in 1762. The Prince, soon to become George IV, wanted it as a proper palace fit for a king. There was already a grand approach road, the Mall, which Charles II had laid out as a wide avenue. Nash built on two side wings facing towards the Mall (they are now hidden by the new front added in 1913). Unfortunately he spent far more money than Parliament had allowed, and got the sack. Another architect completed the work by 1837, just in time for Queen Victoria. Since then it has always been the royal family's main London home.

Cumberland Terrace, one of the streets designed by John Nash.

The capture of the Cato Street Conspirators. In 1820 a group of desperate men plotted to murder the entire Cabinet while they were at dinner. The plot was betrayed, and the gunmen were arrested at their hideaway in Cato Street. You can still see the spot, near Crawford Place by the Edgware Road.

6

Victorian London

Until the nineteenth century London was small enough for people to reach any part they wanted by walking there. They went to work and to school on foot, to the shops, to church and for outings. If goods needed to be delivered, a porter would carry a load on his head and shoulders (unless it was heavy enough to need a cart). You can still see the high porters' rests on the south side of Piccadilly by Green Park.

There were plenty of carriages for hire if you needed one for a special journey. The richest people had their own, kept in the mews at the back of the big houses.

As the population rose, London spread further. Many people found their daily journeys getting longer. Soon it was quite often a question of being too far to walk but too expensive to hire a cab.

George Shilibeer found the answer in Paris: the omnibus. So in 1829 he started London's first regular horse-bus service. It ran every three

One of Shillibeer's Omnibuses. The 'Diorama, Regent's Park' (referred to on the side of the bus) was a show held in a hall behind one of Nash's terraces.

hours in both directions from Paddington Green along the New Road to the Angel, Islington, then south to the Bank of England. Three horses pulled a coach carrying twenty-two passengers.

It was such a success that by 1835 Shillibeer had 600 buses running. Other people copied him. Soon there were buses on all the main streets. Then in 1856 the London General Omnibus Company bought up nearly all the buses and made them into one huge network.

By then a new kind of transport had reached London. The first railway had opened in 1836 from Southwark to Greenwich. It was less than four miles long. In the early days people went on it for the fun of the trip rather than to get to work. But it was cheaper and quicker than a horse bus, and there was a train every fifteen minutes.

At first the railway builders' chief aim was to link the big cities. The London and Birmingham Railway Company laid the first main line to reach the capital in 1837. The huge entrance to its terminus, Euston Station, cost £35 000. Other main lines followed quickly, each with its own London station: Fenchurch Street (1841), Bishopsgate, now Liverpool Street (1847), Waterloo (1848), King's Cross (1852), Paddington (1854), Victoria (1860), St Pancras (1874). These stations stand in a ring round the centre of London. Only one line, built later, went right into the heart of the city. It crossed over Ludgate Hill, and many people thought it was a scandal to have trains blocking the view of St Paul's.

A great many houses had to be pulled down to insert these railway lines through the built-up area of London. On top of that, the stations and goods yards took up many acres of space. Thousands of people lost their homes. Just two miles of track laid by the North London Railway Company cost 900 houses.

The original entrance to Euston Station. The arch was made specially grand and dignified in order to impress travellers. When it was pulled down in 1960 there was a great protest.

Those who lost their homes had to find somewhere else to live. Most of them could only afford to move further out where rents were still reasonable. This often meant going beyond walking distance of their jobs. So the railways were asked to do something to help them. Their answer was Workmen's Penny Trains, running to the main stations early each morning and evening.

Then the railway companies saw that some Londoners might actually choose to move out of the centre. If they could travel into work quickly, they might prefer to live away from the noise and crowds. Stations were opened at the villages which the main lines passed on their routes into London. Places like Wembley, Harrow and Wimbledon suddenly began to expand.

The next step was for a railway company to build a station beside an empty piece of land. Each of these new stations was quickly surrounded by rows of houses. More and more London families wanted their own house and garden and all the homes were sold as soon as they were built. One new station of this type was even called Kingston-on-Railway! (now Surbiton).

London's first Underground was opened to help commuters to get to the City. This Metropolitan Railway, opened in 1863, was nearly four miles long. It linked Paddington, Euston and King's Cross Stations and ran on south eastwards into the City. Later it was joined to the line along the Embankment to form the Inner Circle. London was the first city in the world to have an underground. It was an instant success, far quicker and cheaper than the horse bus.

The Growth of the Suburbs

By the 1860s every main road and railway out of London had new suburbs growing up beside it. London's population was really racing up by now. In 1801 it was 865 000; in 1841 it was 2 million; and by 1901 it reached 4½ million. Only 300 years before, this had been the population of the whole of England.

The London suburbs were growing faster than almost any other place in the country. Soon London was to become the biggest built-up area in the world.

Hundreds of thousands of Victorian houses are still lived in. They form a wide belt round central London (though now there are miles of outer suburb beyond them). Their first owners enjoyed plenty of space and fresh air, since they were next door to open country. At the same time, they could travel quickly to work in central London. The Victorians valued family life very highly. Most working men were content to spend their evenings quietly at home with their wives and children.

Slowly the population of inner London started

The first journey on the Metropolitan Railway. The Metropolitan Railway was an instant success. It was so much faster and cheaper than the omnibus that the passengers were willing to put up with the smoke and noise.

to fall. Houses were pulled down, shops and offices took their place. All the time more Londoners moved out to places like Brixton, Highbury and Ealing.

Land-owners and builders made fortunes providing all these new homes. Anyone who owned farm land or a big garden close to London had the chance of selling it for building. Most owners sold or leased their land to building firms who did the actual work. In South London leases were very often for eighty years. At the end of that time, the children of the original owner got back the land. Only now it was covered with houses and worth a great deal more. Very few people could afford to buy their new home outright. Building Societies were fairly rare. So most of the houses were let for monthly rents.

The demand was so great that as soon as a new road was laid and house plans drawn, people started snapping up the houses. Most of the new suburbs consisted of semi-detached pairs and rows of houses. Developers sometimes sold single houses, but you could not pack so many homes into a small space that way. The decoration varies, but the basic shape of these houses is usually the same. A front door led into the hall, with a living room beside it. Often there was a second living room at the back, and a scullery added on behind. Upstairs came front and back bedrooms, and another one over the scullery. Often there was another floor above this. A great many houses were like this only one size larger. There might be a basement with a kitchen and servants' room in it, and a fourth (attic) floor at the top. In the nineteenth century the majority of families with a house to themselves would employ at least one servant.

Almost all these London houses were built of brick. Yellowish grey stock brick was the most common, but there is plenty of red brick as well. The roofs were usually welsh slate. All kinds of plaster mouldings were used to decorate the porches and windows. Bay windows became very popular towards the end of the century.

There were plenty of books of house designs. They had titles like *The Handy Book of Villa Architecture*. Here the builder could pick patterns for every part of the house, inside and out. Doors, fireplaces, ceilings, bannisters—they were more solid and more highly decorated than they would be today.

The Public Health Act of 1875 laid down a basic quality for new houses. Walls had to be more than a certain thickness and there had to be a damp course, a flush lavatory and proper drains. Each house had to have a sink with running water (but not hot water yet), and a copper for boiling clothes.

If you were going to get as many houses along each street as before the Act, each house had to be long and narrow. On a 14–17 foot (4–5 metres) frontage, the scullery, coalshed and lavatory had to be added one behind the other at the back.

Meanwhile far larger houses were being built in the fashionable inner suburbs. Belgrave Square (finished in 1837) gave the name Belgravia to the area west of Buckingham Palace. Beyond it, Knightsbridge and Kensington were filling up with rows of elegant new houses.

One reason why these houses seem so large is that the ceilings are very high. This is because the new gas lamps gave off so much heat. They were first used for street lighting in 1807, but did not become common for lighting houses till the 1860s. Gas fires and gas cookers were still in the future. Every room in these houses had a coal fire which needed daily cleaning. There were big iron ranges in the kitchens which also burned coal. If you look at the roofs of these houses you will see dozens of chimney pots. Imagine smoke pouring out of every chimney. On still days the smoke hung over London in a dense blanket. Often it made its way down to street level, into every cranny, up people's nostrils. These were the days of the awful pea-souper fogs when you could not see more than a metre or two in front of you.

The Slums

The old houses still left in central London got shabbier and more crowded. Many of them were built over cess-pits. People got their water from a public pump which only ran for a short while each day. No one cared about the slums till there were outbreaks of cholera and typhus in 1831 and 1837. The first victims lived in the dirtiest and most over-crowded parts of London. Then richer

A Lodging house in Fish Lane, Holborn, about 1840. It was in houses like this that cholera and typhoid broke out. There is an open sewer running directly under the floor.

'Nearly the whole of the labouring population have only one room. The corpse is therefore kept in that room where the inmates sleep and have their meals. Sometimes the corpse is stretched on the bed . . . and the wife and family lie on the floor.'

people fell ill too, and blamed the slums for hatching disease.

Parliament asked a lawyer, called Edwin Chadwick to investigate. He went into the poorest districts with his notebook ready. Everywhere he asked questions, watched, measured and sniffed. Finally in 1842 he wrote a report which shocked many people.

Chadwick's 'Report on the Sanitary condition of the Labouring Population' included descriptions like this one about death in Whitechapel:

As a result of the Report, Parliament set up a Central Board of Health. Chadwick was in charge, but the Board had very little power. Many districts were very slow to take the Board's advice on how they could improve their slums. Every slum house, every bad drain and every careless water company had a private owner. None of these people would budge an inch unless they were forced to. In spite of Chadwick's pleas, Parliament refused to do this.

No one should have been surprised when there was another big cholera outbreak in 1848. More and more people were sure that bad housing, rotten drains and impure water were the cause. They noticed that most of the victims lived in south London. No wonder—their drinking water was pumped from the Thames almost opposite central London's main sewer outlet! This was on the north bank of the Thames near Charing Cross. Each parish along the river poured in its filth as well.

By this time London had the reputation of being the smelliest capital in Europe. But help was on the way: in 1848 the Metropolitan Commissioners of Sewers were appointed. They replaced eight separate bodies responsible for London's drains, and began work on a new plan.

Plan after plan was brought out and turned down. Another ten years passed with nothing achieved. Then the summer of 1858 was specially hot and dry. Buildings close to the river smelt so awful that people could hardly bear to go into them. At low tide the mud banks were strewn with solid sewage. Workmen went out with lime and carbolic to try to cover it up. Londoners nick-named that summer 'The Great Stink'.

By now everyone agreed that something drastic must be done. Sir Joseph Bazalgette (chief engineer of the Metropolitan Commission of Sewers)

The opening of London's new sewage works in 1865. The Prince of Wales pressed the switch to start them working. With its gothic columns, the works was so splendid that it became a show-place for foreign visitors.

had his master plan accepted at last. First he built two new main sewers parallel to the Thames, one on each side of the river. All the existing drains which now flowed into the river would run into these instead. The new sewers took their load downstream to new sewage works at Barking and Crossness. Finally, it was discharged in the Thames far down towards the sea.

At last the Thames began to get cleaner. Sir Joseph Bazagette also began the great task of replacing the old brick sewers with more efficient tile-lined versions.

There was still the smelly mud to deal with (though it was far less unpleasant now that the sewage outlets were cut off). Sir Joseph had been appointed Chief Engineer to the new Metropolitan Board of Works (started in 1855), and he took charge of the building of new streets.

What he planned was an embankment all along the north bank of the Thames from Blackfriars to Westminster. First a granite wall was built out in the river. Then earth was brought from Hampstead to fill in the area between the wall and the river bank. Care was taken to leave space in it for an extra sewer and gas, electricity and water pipes. There was also room for an underground railway (later part of the Inner Circle). A broad road was laid on top of all this. There was room for new buildings and public gardens as well. London had gained 37 extra acres and a quick east–west route, the Victoria Embankment. Later there was an embankment built further up river towards Chelsea, and another across the Thames by Lambeth.

London's first electric street lights were tried out on the Victoria Embankment in 1878. They consisted of carbon rods, but soon modern filament bulbs were used. The demand for electricity grew quickly as people saw how clean and simple it was. Ten years later the first big power station was opened at Deptford.

The deathrate fell with better drains and purer water to drink. But many of the filthy and rotting houses were still lived in. People who were very poor could not possibly afford to move to the new suburbs. The old houses just got more and more crowded, and it was left to a few private citizens to do something on their own.

Two voluntary housing societies were started

Cleopatra's Needle being erected on the Victoria Embankment. This was a gift to Britain from the government of Egypt. For years it lay in the desert sand, too heavy and expensive to move. Finally the money was raised to bring the Needle to England. It arrived in 1878 and was placed beside the river steps in front of the Adelphi.

in 1849 and 1850. They built blocks of flats in central London to give people decent homes at a low rent. (One of these blocks is still standing in Streatham Street, near Oxford Circus.) Each flat had a small hall, living room, two bedrooms, a scullery and a lavatory.

Then George Peabody, a rich American, paid for twenty-nine blocks of flats out of his own pocket. The first was opened in 1864 in Commercial Street, Spitalfields. This also provided three-room flats, with shared laundries and toilet facilities. Some of the Peabody Buildings are still in use, though they have had to be modernized inside.

Octavia Hill had far less cash than Peabody, but she collected money to buy a few run-down houses. She did them up and let them to poor families at a low rent. By 1875 there were 26 000 Londoners living in flats or houses run by private

housing trusts. Yet this was only a tiny fraction of those in need. Several housing companies tried to build estates for working people. But if they charged a rent which covered their costs, poor families could not afford them. In the end it was Council housing which was to provide the answer, but that did not get properly under way till the twentieth century.

Some people did not even have a share of one room. Many slept in the open, or in odd corners and alleyways. One boy made himself a bed inside a huge iron roller in Regent's Park! In 1850 about a quarter of London's population could not earn enough money to buy food and clothes all through the year. They had to ask for help from their district Poor Law officials. Usually they were offered a place in the local workhouse (a new act in 1834 made sure that every group of parishes had a workhouse). Here they were given a bed in a dormitory; husbands, wives and children were all kept apart. The food was mostly soup, porridge and bread, with meat only once a week.

People would struggle on cold and hungry rather than go into such a place. An author called Henry Mayhew wrote about how people as poor as this managed to live. He spoke to dozens of them and turned their answers into a book called *London Labour and the London Poor* in 1861. There was the little girl who sold matches at a street corner, earning 6d a week. A crippled young man crawled along on his knees with nutmeg graters hung round his neck (his hands were deformed too). People like this often shared a filthy bed in a basement. They never had new clothes or a proper meal.

Lord Shaftesbury was another man who cared about poor people in distress. Like Chadwick, he wanted Parliament to pass laws to help them. He put forward a law to stop young children working in factories; another to reduce the working hours of all workers; another to prevent small boys being sent up chimneys as sweeps. Shaftesbury always made a good case to the other members of Parliament. He brought poor boys to his house to answer their questions and describe how they lived. Like Mayhew and Chadwick, he had gone into the slums to find things out for himself.

Charles Dickens also told the well-off Victorians about those who were less fortunate. But he did it in a different way—through his novels. As a boy he had worked in a small factory which made black polish to put on boots. The dirty, cramped workrooms, the long hours and the cruel boss are all described in *David Copperfield*. Thus his readers would find out how a great many Londoners spent their working time. Dickens

also wrote some of the most vivid descriptions of London streets, crowded with carriages and lit by gas lamps. He used all his skill to give his reader the very feel, smell and sound of London.

New Streets and New Squares

Regent Street and its extensions was the biggest piece of town planning in London in the eighteenth century. Nash had another bold idea as soon as it was finished. This was to build a large square at the top of Whitehall, just north of Charing Cross. At that time the space was occupied by the Royal Mews (stables). Parliament agreed to Nash's plan in 1826, and by 1830 the area had been cleared. Now it was given a name— Trafalgar Square. Then someone suggested it would be the ideal site for a national memorial to Lord Nelson. It took three years to build the 170-foot (52 metres) column and the huge statue of Nelson himself to go on top of it. The lions at the base were added later, and the fountains later still.

The north side of Trafalgar Square made a good site for the new National Gallery. Pillars

Northumberland House being pulled down in 1875. The Duke of Northumberland tried to prevent it, the public protested. But the Metropolitan Board of Works was able to force the sale of the house to make room for its new road to the Embankment.

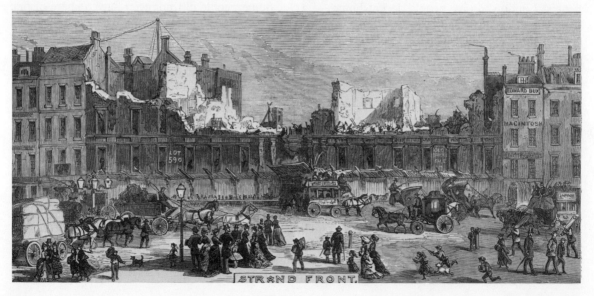

STRAND FRONT.

84

from the Prince Regent's old home, Carlton House, were used to make a striking front for it.

South-east of the square stood Northumberland House; at least it did until 1874. Then this splendid seventeenth-century mansion was pulled down, the last of the great houses along the Strand. A dreary street of offices and hotels was built on the site (use a map to find out what it is called). The red lion which once stood above the gate was moved to Syon House at Isleworth (another home of the Dukes of Northumberland).

The new road linked Trafalgar Square with the Embankment. Several other new streets were built to make it easier to get across central London. Victorians suffered from traffic jams almost as much as we do now. Most of these streets were cleverly placed to run through the sites of the worst slums. This meant that the land for the new street was cheap to buy, and the slums were due to be pulled down anyway.

Victoria Street was one of the earliest. It was begun in 1852 and ran eastwards from West-minster Abbey. Beside it are some of the first purpose-built flats in London (these were large flats for well-off families, quite different from the Peabody Buildings).

New Oxford Street replaced the worst slum of all, known as the Rookery. This was round St Giles-in-the-Fields, where the 1665 plague had started. The new road was never a success like the old Oxford Street. Few people risked opening a smart shop here; to this day it is not a place which attracts shoppers.

Shaftesbury Avenue and Charing Cross Road were cut through an area of terrible slums in 1886–7. Piccadilly Circus was enlarged to join the southern end of Shaftesbury Avenue (this meant it was no longer a true circus, which should be round). When Lord Shaftesbury died, this was the place chosen for his memorial. The sculptor wanted his statue to remind people how Lord Shaftesbury had cared for his fellow men. So he carved Cupid, the god of love, with an arrow fitted ready in his bow. At once a newspaper nick-named the statue 'Eros', the Greek word for love. And so it has been called ever since.

Traffic jams were just as bad in the City as in the West End. So Queen Victoria Street was built to provide a broad, straight route across its

New London Bridge being built beside the old. The 'starlings' are still there, though the houses on the bridge had been pulled down many years earlier.

southern half. This did not run through slums, but it replaced a maze of small streets.

New bridges also helped to make traffic flow more easily. Old London bridge was rebuilt at last in 1831–4. King William Street and Moor-gate Street, both new, made it easier to reach the bridge from the north.

Many of the new bridges were built to carry railways, not roads. They brought trains right into London, to Blackfriars, Charing Cross, Cannon Street and Victoria Stations. More and more people lived out along the southern lines now. They came by train to within walking distance of their offices in the City.

The final new bridge of the nineteenth century was Tower Bridge. It lies further downstream than any other bridge, so it needs to open to allow large ships through. The gothic towers were designed to match the Tower of London close by. Inside there is modern machinery to lift the central section of the roadway.

Entertainments

In Victorian London people from different social classes did not see much of each other. Even in their free time the classes went their separate ways. Richer Londoners liked going out to the theatre, and many men still spent a lot of time at their clubs. Working people preferred music halls, and went to the local pub in the evening.

Victorian pubs stood out much more than

A Victorian public house: the Bombay Grab in Bow Road.

modern ones. Bright lights, golden lettering and large windows all helped to draw in the customers. No wonder many people came here night after night to enjoy the beer, warmth and good company. Inside there was plenty of polished wood and gleaming mirrors.

Victorian music halls started from singsongs in pubs. Then the best singers turned professional. Special theatres were built. Most of them served drinks, and even meals, while the show was going on. All sorts of variety acts were put on, as well as the songs, to make a good evening's show. Wilton's in Whitechapel, Canterbury Hall, Lambeth, and the Bedford, Camden Town, were among the most famous of the old Music Halls.

Serious plays were quite rare in the early nineteenth century. Till 1843 there was a ban on showing plays without music; only two theatres had a licence to do it. The two theatres were very big to hold as many people as possible. Some of the audience would be so far from the stage that they could hardly see the actors' faces. Everything had to be very crude and brightly lit to show up. Subtle acting was wasted in such a huge theatre.

Playgoers at this time liked very elaborate sets, rich costumes and fairy-tale plots. No one went to the theatre to see a slice of everyday life. You went to see a fantasy like a poor factory girl marrying a rich lord.

In the 1880s there was a great burst of new theatre building. A whole row of theatres appeared in the new Shaftesbury Avenue. By the 1890s London had more theatres than any other city in the world (thirty-eight in the centre plus twenty-three in the suburbs). These new theatres were much more comfortable than the earlier ones. The audiences were also much more demanding about seeing a really well-written play.

Famous actors raised standards, people like Henry Irving at the Lyceum Theatre, and Beerbohm Tree at Her Majesty's in Haymarket. Brilliant playwrights such as Oscar Wilde were at work. For family outings, Gilbert and Sullivan operas were all the rage. Richard D'Oyley Carte had built a special theatre for them, the Savoy.

Football and cricket were becoming more popular by this time. Properly laid out sports grounds were a new feature of London now. Turf taken from Tooting Common was used to make a cricket ground at Kennington. Here the first Test Match was played in 1880. It had already

A Victorian Music Hall. The audience enjoys a meal while the show goes on.

been used for its other game, football; the cup final took place here in 1871.

Saturday afternoon closing of offices meant a change in the family week-end. People started coming to the West End from the suburbs to shop. Or they might spend their free afternoon window-gazing or visiting a museum or a show. In good weather the parks and commons were favourite places to go. Hyde Park and Regent's Park (both owned by the Crown) were safe for all time. But with building land in such demand, some open spaces were in danger. Much of Wandsworth Common was sold to developers to build houses. The owner of the manor of Hampstead tried to put up an estate on Hampstead Heath. He was stopped, but only after a long battle. The Metropolitan Board of Works bought the Heath in 1871 and gave it to the public. Battersea Park had been opened in the 1850s, and Victoria Park, Hackney was opened to celebrate Queen Victoria's silver jubilee in 1863.

The Great Exhibition of 1851

The greatest single show of the nineteenth century was the Great Exhibition of 1851 (its centenary was celebrated in 1951 by the Festival of Britain). By now England's industry led the world. A group of people led by Prince Albert decided to hold a huge exhibition to show everyone what Britain could make. Other countries were invited to send examples of their work too.

For such a huge show, a really enormous building was needed. The site chosen was the biggest open space handy for central London: Hyde Park. Over 200 designs for an exhibition hall were considered and all turned down by Prince Albert and his committee. Finally, Joseph Paxton (who was the Duke of Devonshire's gardener) drew a sketch of a huge greenhouse on some blotting paper. The committee was shown it, liked it, and asked Paxton to turn it into a proper design.

Work started the moment the plan was finished. The 'Crystal Palace' was made of hundreds of steel girders and thousands of panes of glass. It was a third of a mile long, and tall enough to enclose the trees in the park.

It was ready in four months. Now the 100 000

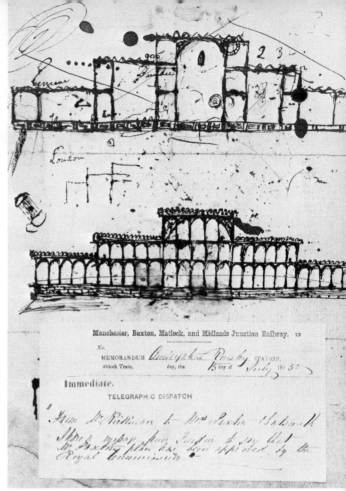

Joseph Paxton's blotting paper sketch for the Great Exhibition.

exhibits from all over the world began to arrive. They ranged from huge objects like railway engines to tiny pieces of jewellery. People poured into London to see it from all over England and beyond. Special trains brought day trippers; Mr Thomas Cook first made his name organizing party visits. London's hotels were overflowing. In fact many people camped out in the fine weather. Queen Victoria wrote to her uncle after the official opening 'I wish you could have witnessed the 1st. May 1851, the greatest day in our history, the most beautiful and imposing and touching spectacle ever seen'. Six million tickets were sold between May and October, when it closed.

At the end of the exhibition the great halls were taken down. Hyde Park's grass and trees were out in the open once more, and there is no mark where the palace once stood. (In fact it ran

The Crystal Palace, after it had been moved out to Sydenham.

parallel to Knightsbridge, with the main entrance opposite Ennismore Gardens.) Just under the grass there are still concrete foundations where the main supporting arches stood.

The Brighton Railway Company bought the Crystal Palace and rebuilt it at Sydenham. Here it stood, used as an exhibition and concert hall, until it was burnt down in 1936. The park here is still named after it.

The Great Exhibition had made a large profit. Most of this money was used to buy a site just south of Hyde Park. Here a whole complex of museums and colleges was gradually built. The South Kensington Museum (later rebuilt and re-named the Victoria and Albert Museum) was the first. Meanwhile another large exhibition was held in 1862, on the Cromwell Road. When that

was dismantled, the Natural History Museum went up in its place. (The parts of this exhibition building went to north London to make the Alexandra Palace at Muswell Hill. Only sixteen days after its official opening in 1873 it burnt down, and had to be rebuilt in brick. It was never such a success as the Crystal Palace.)

The road which runs south from Knightsbridge to Cromwell Road is still called Exhibition Road. At right angles runs Prince Consort Road, named in honour of Prince Albert. Just north of it there is the Albert Hall, still London's biggest concert hall. But poor Albert did not live long enough to see all these plans complete. When he died in 1861 Queen Victoria ordered a memorial to be built. It stands in Hyde Park, just opposite the Albert Hall.

Commercial London: Shops and Docks

By 1870 Britain had by far the biggest overseas trade of any country in the world. Not only luxuries were imported now. As the population grew, more and more food had to be brought in from other countries. Raw materials were needed as well, to supply Britain's expanding factories.

Britain was still exporting cloth to pay for all this. But by now she had also become the greatest supplier of machinery to the rest of the world. Her iron and steel furnaces provided railway engines, ships, saucepans, bedsteads—anything made of metal one could possibly think of.

This meant that by mid-century new docks were again needed. In 1855 the Victoria Dock was opened below Blackwall. It was joined to the Thames by locks. This kept the water deep in the dock even when it was low tide in the river outside. The Royal Albert Dock was added beside it in 1880, providing for even bigger ships.

Ships coming to these docks still had to wait for high tide to sail in. Yet with a quick rail service, it no longer mattered if the docks were some distance from central London. So Tilbury Docks were begun in 1886. These are far enough down river for ships to be able to reach them at any stage of the tide. Gradually most of the ocean-going ships began to dock here.

New warehouses were built to store all the goods going and coming from London. Most of them are shabby and unused now, but when they were new, plenty of ships still came to unload just below London Bridge. There were specially large numbers of coal boats. These put their cargoes into 'lighters' to be ferried ashore at small quays all along the river front. Everyone heated their houses and did their cooking with coal. By 1875 London was using eight million tons a year. But by then more and more of it was coming in by rail and canal instead of by sea.

Some of the new cargoes were much more tricky to handle than the old. Food might perish if it was stored for long. Vinegar and salt were in great demand for preserving food. Then in the 1880s the first refrigerated ships arrived from Australia and New Zealand. At once new cold store warehouses were needed.

With so many more customers, shops were expanding too. Plate glass windows first appeared early in the century. A draper's shop in Ludgate Hill was the first to install a really large one. Other drapers quickly followed its example. Suddenly the art of window dressing became more important. Victorian shop windows were usually crammed with goods and posters. The skill lay in getting as many things on show as possible. Before self-service, it was useful to know what prices a shop was charging before stepping inside.

There were still some big shops in the City in Victorian times. But the new and smarter shops were opening in the West End. Here you could find shops selling all sorts of goods under one roof. The Soho Bazaar in Soho Square and the Pantheon in Oxford Street were two of these early general stores for 'fancy goods'. But the first real purpose-built department store was the Bon Marché, opened in Brixton in 1877.

People came to look as much as to buy. They also came to meet their friends. When the Army and Navy Stores opened in Victoria Street in 1871, the people living nearby used it as a club as well as a shop.

Whiteley's in Westbourne Grove was another early department store which is still going strong. Queen Victoria used to order her children's toys from here. Harrods had started as a small grocer's shop in 1849; by 1900 it had eighty departments. By that time Knightsbridge and

Peter Jones' Department Store, Sloane Square, Chelsea, about 1900. Peter Jones' shop still stands on the same site, though it has been rebuilt in a modern style.

Kensington High Street had developed as a big shopping area.

If all this sounds very modern, remember that the herding of live cattle in London streets went on till 1867! Then the live meat market opened in Caledonian Road; after that Smithfield only dealt in carcases. Fresh fruit and vegetables were still sold mainly from barrows. Pineapples were first seen in the streets of London in 1842 and quickly became popular. Great quantities of oranges were sold by street sellers.

The large market hall at Covent Garden (built in 1828–30) was no longer big enough. Thirty years later the Floral Hall was put up alongside. Here all London's wholesale flower, fruit and vegetable trade was carried on till it moved to Nine Elms in 1974.

For most Londoners, shopping meant the daily visit to the local grocer and the butcher. (Many richer families had food delivered direct to the house; the butcher and baker would call each day for orders.) The Victorian grocer had great boxes and barrels, full of things which we buy ready made up into packets. He weighed out your sugar, flour, tea, butter, bacon and cheese, in just the amount you needed. The shops had a pleasant smell all their own, which you never find in a supermarket.

The General Post Office in St Martin-le-Grand. Sir Robert Smirke designed London's main post office, near St Paul's. Each evening at 8 o'clock coaches left the post office to deliver letters all over England. Soon the railways replaced them, and this building was also rebuilt, and finally pulled down.

Public Buildings

All through the nineteenth century there was plenty of money to pay for large public buildings. They were very solidly built, and many of them are still in use. In the first forty years the classical style was still in fashion. The outside design of all these buildings is fairly similar. Most of them have a big central portico and balancing side wings (often with pillars along them also). Inside, the buildings have all sorts of different uses.

Sir Robert Smirke designed the British Museum, the Mint, the Customs House, the General Post Office and King's College. Another architect working at this time was William Wilkins. He designed the National Gallery, University College and St George's Hospital, Hyde Park Corner. On the whole, his buildings are longer and lower than Smirke's, and he liked to put on a dome. They have the same portico and side wings. As with Smirke, you could not tell from the outside which of these buildings was a museum or a hospital, a college or a post office.

Unlike the Georgians, the Victorians did not just borrow their ideas for designs from one classical source. In fact they considered the long rows of square-windowed, simple eighteenth-century houses very dull. They wanted their buildings to stand out from all these plain terraces.

The Victorians borrowed styles from all over the world and from every age. When architects were designing clubs for Pall Mall, they based them on sixteenth-century Italian palaces. When William Waterhouse was planning the Natural History Museum, he copied the outside of a German early medieval cathedral.

Later in Victoria's reign it was the Gothic style which became the great favourite. This was a revival of the late medieval style with its pointed arches, turrets and spires. John Ruskin was one of its pioneers. He hated mass-produced factory goods. Instead he turned back to the hand-made craftsmanship of the medieval builders. He encouraged young architects to take their sketchbooks into country churches. Here they carefully drew all the details put there five or six hundred years before. Then they built churches as like them as possible; these are known as 'Gothic

Revival' churches. You find them all over London and all over England.

The first buildings which really made 'Gothic Revival' famous were the new Houses of Parliament. The old Palace of Westminster had burnt down in a terrible fire in 1834. There was no proper fire brigade yet (it was started in 1866 after a run of big fires). Soldiers tried to stop the blaze, but only Westminster Hall was saved. Here fire engines were taken right indoors to pump jets of water onto the wooden roof from below.

The competition for a new Houses of Parliament was won by a young man called Charles Barry. Barry wanted to build it in the classical style, which was still in fashion, but the MPS insisted in Gothic. They wanted the new building to remind them of the old medieval one. So Barry went to Belgium to look at its famous medieval town halls. Then he asked his friend Pugin, an expert on early art, to decorate the new building.

Poor Barry worked himself to death on the Houses of Parliament. The MPS kept on arguing and changing their minds. Barry started work at six each morning, taking only a few hours sleep. After his death, his son finished the work. The

great clock tower, Big Ben, was one of the last parts to be completed. The huge bell cracked while it was being hoisted into place. So did the second, but it was too expensive to replace it again. You can still hear the slightly harsh sound which Big Ben makes when it strikes the hour.

Gothic caught on fast. By the 1870s, private houses were being built with arched windows and porches. The competition for a new building for the Law Courts was won by a Gothic design (in 1868). The judges never thought about the people who would have to work in it; they just wanted an imposing outside. The Law Courts have splendid towers, a grand hall like a church, and a striking roof line; but many of the offices are dark and poky.

Architects would turn their hand to any style their clients asked for. In 1856 Sir George Gilbert Scott designed new government offices for Whitehall in the Gothic style. But the Prime Minister, Lord Palmerston, did not like them. He asked Scott to change the outside to look like an Italian sixteenth century palace. So Scott did as he was asked.

Years later Scott designed St Pancras Station and its huge hotel, all in the Gothic style. His rivals said he had just taken the old government office plans out of a drawer and adapted them. It is certainly very ornate for a railway station. Even the ticket office has linen-fold panelling.

The Gothic style could be used for anything now. The new Prudential Assurance offices in Holborn had slit windows and turrets, all in bright red shiny bricks. Styles were beginning to get mixed up. You found churches being built in the Gothic shape, but out of red brick (such as All Saints', Margaret Street). Houses and offices might have features borrowed from several different styles to suit the client's fancy. The Imperial Institute, designed by Colcutt in 1893, was a mixture of Flemish, French and Spanish styles. Nearby, W. S. Gilbert's home in Harrington Gardens was based on a Dutch merchant's house with stepped gables. Some of the big new hotels, such as the Charing Cross and the Grosvenor, had a taste of a French castle about them.

Towards the end of the century some people began to get tired of all this decoration. Even if

The Law Courts in the Strand. George Street won the competition to design the new building in 1868. Before this, the courts had met in very cramped conditions in Westminster Hall. These are the main courts where disputes over wills, divorces and business deals are tried; they are not criminal courts.

Charing Cross Hotel. The station and hotel were built in 1863 on the site of the old Hungerford Market. A large gothic-style cross was put up in the station forecourt at the same time. It is close to the site of Edward I's cross, marking the last resting place of his wife's coffin on its journey to Westminster. Notice the gas lamps and the iron railings.

these newer buildings showed up well (especially through a fog) the old Georgian houses were more restful to look at. The Queen Anne style began to come into fashion. Norman Shaw designed the New Scotland Yard building in this style. He was to be one of the most fashionable architects by the turn of the century.

Schools and Colleges

London, like the rest of England, had no state schools till after 1870. There were plenty of private schools. There were also a few older schools like Westminster and St Paul's. But for most children the only chance of a school place was at a church school. Two church societies had been set up to run schools in the early nineteenth century. They were very short of money, and were run rather like factories. The best known in London was the Borough Road School, run by the British and Foreign Schools Society. The government gave money to these two societies to open more schools. Yet there were nothing like enough of them to give every child a place. Lord Shaftesbury helped set up what were called Ragged Schools for the poorest children. Here you got a free dinner as well as free lessons.

At last, in 1870, Parliament passed an Act giving the go-ahead for the first state schools. The rate payers in every town had to choose people to form a school board. These boards would build and run the new schools. London was given one London School Board for all the built-up area. Many of the schools it built are still used. The first one was opened in 1873 in Old Castle Street, Whitechapel. All these schools have a badge on the wall with the initials LSB and the date it was built. Some elderly people still call primary schools 'Board Schools' because they went to one of them.

The architect chosen by the London School Board liked the Queen Anne style. To save space, boys, girls and infants were all put into one building for each district. Often these are three or four floors high. Many have the tall Dutch gables which the architect also admired. There was usually a hall in the middle for prayers and gym, with classrooms leading off it.

Private schools followed a similar plan. Some of the old schools were rebuilt (St Paul's moved to Hammersmith and a girls' school was started close by). The Girls' Public Day School Trust started schools in the middle-class suburbs. South Hampstead High School, built in 1878, is one of these. It has a steep gable in front and there are classrooms leading off the hall.

London at last got its own university in the nineteenth century. Until then, Oxford and Cambridge were the only universities in England, and you had to belong to the Church of England to go to them. University College was founded in

Children in the playground at Montem Street School. No school would be built like this today. What are the main disadvantages of schools like this, of which many are still in use?

1826, and its classical building is described on p. 90. In the hallway you can see the skeleton of Jeremy Bentham, left to the College in his will. It was his ideas which led men like Chadwick to try to improve life for deprived people.

King's College also has a grand building, in one wing of Somerset House in the Strand. Later in the century several other colleges were founded, such as the London School of Economics and Imperial College. You can study any subject under the sun in London. There are colleges for art, music, every kind of craft and language. Many of these are attached to London University, making it Britain's biggest university by far.

Yet perhaps more people learnt things for themselves in the British Museum than anywhere else in London. By Queen Victoria's time the old museum in Montagu House was filled to bursting. The Elgin Marbles had arrived from Greece in 1816; George IV had given the royal library of 120 000 books to the nation. The new museum was built all round the old house. When it was finished, the treasures were moved into their new home and Montagu House was pulled down.

This left an empty space in the middle. The Keeper of Printed Books, Antonio Panizzi, saw how it could be used. He designed a round reading room under a huge dome. Here thousands of books could be stored. In the centre there was desk space for hundreds of readers. A great many famous writers and scholars have worked here in the British Museum Reading Room.

Change and Protest

London's old methods of town government could not cope with her vast growth. The City went on running its own affairs through its Common Council, but the rest of the built-up area was still controlled by dozens of separate parish authorities. What was really needed was one big council to cover the whole area. A giant city needed altogether new methods of control. A new word, 'metropolis', was used to describe it.

The Metropolitan Commissioners of Sewers (started in 1848) was a first step. Its main job was to run the new road-building programme. Progress went on bit by bit; the Metropolitan

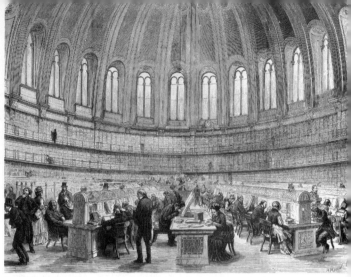

Inside the reading room of the British Museum.

Fire Brigade started in 1866. The Metropolitan Water Act of 1871 gave some public control over water supplies (though the Metropolitan Water Board was not created till early next century). Gradually the needs of the great city were being provided for by these new bodies. But a government inquiry showed much corruption, and the jobs were not always properly done. Finally, in 1888, the London County Council was started. At last London had one elected council to look after every part of the running of the metropolis.

All this had been achieved without riots or revolutions. Yet London had seen some huge demonstrations during the nineteenth century. Most were about national politics, where feelings seem to run higher. The Chartists had held monster meetings in the 1840s but there was no violence. An angry crowd tore down the railings in Hyde Park at a protest meeting in 1866. But this had had a good result—the creation of Speakers' Corner.

Life improved for ordinary people as the country got richer. It was not till the slump of the 1880s that there were ugly scenes again. In 1886 2000 unemployed men stormed through the West End carrying red flags. They threw stones at the windows of the rich men's clubs in Pall Mall and St James's. Worse happened the next year. This was in November 1887. 100 000 people marched from Clerkenwell to Trafalgar Square to demand jobs and fair pay. The police called in soldiers with fixed bayonets to break up the crowd. Eleanor, daughter of Karl Marx, was

The boundaries of the London County Council (1888) and Greater London Council (1965).

there and wrote 'I was in the thick of the fight at Parliament Street and afterwards in Northumberland Avenue. I got pretty roughly used myself'.

Neither of these marches won anything from the government. But in the following year, London's first successful dock strike was held. The men marched through London with their leader, Ben Tillett, to win support for their demand for 6d an hour. They carried pieces of mouldy bread and meat, telling passers-by that this was all they could afford. There were mass meetings on Tower Hill and in Trafalgar Square. These were completely orderly, and public opinion came over to the dockers' side. In the end the owners gave way and paid the 6d wage.

By now a larger organization had been formed to try to get workers better wages and conditions. The Trades Union Congress had grown out of the London Trades Council in 1868. It looked as if union action, not mass marches, would achieve their aims in future.

In this, as in so many other ways, the Victorians had learnt by their mistakes. They had had to cope with a city larger than there had ever been anywhere before. Its quick growth had brought much hardship to many people. Yet by 1900 London was coping reasonably well with its vast problems. For most of its citizens it provided decent homes, clean streets, schools, hospitals, public transport—in fact all the machinery for modern life in a metropolis.

Questions on Victorian London

1 Describe a journey on Shillibeer's horse bus from Paddington Green to the Bank of England.
2 A Victorian family is trying to decide whether or not to move out to the suburbs. What arguments might they use for and against the move?
3 Why were there outbreaks of cholera and typhus in Victorian London?
4 Find the new streets made through central London slums in the nineteenth century, and mark them on a sketch map.
5 Describe how a visitor came to London by train in 1851 and went to see the Great Exhibition.
6 Make a list of any Victorian houses, churches, pubs and schools you can find in your part of London. Choose one of them, and try to see how much of it is original, and what has been altered or added later.

7
London in the Twentieth Century

If you set off north or south from Charing Cross in 1900, you reached open country in about eight miles. Since then London has made another great outward surge. Now there is a huge ring of newer suburbs beyond the ones the Victorians built.

By 1939 new houses were eating up farmland as far out as fifteen miles from Charing Cross. Some people began to realize the danger of this sprawl. If it went on, London would become a very unpleasant place to live in. So County Councils on the borders of the London area started to buy up fields and woods to stop them being built over. They aimed to make a Green Belt all round. But they did not have enough money to buy more than a few acres here and there.

Then came the Second World War, and for five years all building stopped. Aferwards people were willing to accept much more firm control by the state. The Town and Country Planning Act of 1947 said that no buildings could be put up without the official planners' consent. It meant London could keep the builders away and create a proper Green Belt. It was not a complete ring of open country and it varied in width. But it finally stopped London's outward spread.

By the time the halt came, thousands of acres of farmland had been covered with houses. The demand for new homes was just as strong in the twentieth century as in the nineteenth since so many people came to London to take up new jobs. The number of men in government offices, banks and businesses was racing up. They earned good salaries and could afford new houses in the suburbs.

The pre-1914 houses are more cheerful and less heavy looking than the Victorian ones. Fewer people could afford servants, so there were smaller rooms and fewer of them.

As well as the people new to London, there were plenty of families moving because they wanted somewhere more comfortable to live. They almost always moved further out in the same direction: east Londoners to Ilford, north Londoners to Palmers Green, west Londoners to

An advertisement from 'Metroland', published in 1925 by the Metropolitan Railway Company to encourage people to move out into the north west suburbs.

Ealing, for example. It was very rare for families to move across the River Thames.

After the First World War people hoped that the standard of living was going to rise for everyone. Soldiers coming back from the Front were promised 'Homes fit for Heroes'; but it was not easy to provide them. Wages were much higher than before the war. So were the prices of bricks, tiles and wood. It now cost four times as much to build a house as it had in 1914. The government offered to help pay for both public and private housing. But private builders only started work on a big scale when costs began to fall from 1923 onwards.

Building societies now began to grow; a cash deposit (usually 10% of the cost of a house) was put down and the building society lent the other 90%. The new owner repaid this loan (or mortgage) over about twenty years. At last people with small incomes were given a chance to buy their own homes.

Builders were quick to provide for this new market. Sites were cheaper now as so many farmers could not make a living. Thousands more semi-detached houses went up all round London. Most of them had three bedrooms and two living rooms, plus kitchen and bathroom. Usually a building firm did not use an architect. It was cheaper to work out a simple plan without one. All sorts of decorations were added on to attract customers. Strips of timber gave the Tudor cottage look; pieces of stained glass in front windows; pillars to hold up porches—they all helped to make a house a bit different from the one next door. But under the frills the houses were nearly all the same. The new estates were just as dull as the Victorian ones had been.

House prices began to come down in the 1930s, so many builders had to compete to sell their wares. They spent a lot of money on advertising and one of the houses on a new estate would be furnished as a show house. Cheap cars were coming on the market so many homes were now built with a garage attached.

Meanwhile, homes in central London grew more and more expensive. By 1900 no private landlord could afford to build homes for poor people in the centre. But many people *had* to live in the centre because of their work. Dockers, market workers, hotel staff and others all needed to live within walking distance of their jobs. So more and more people packed into the existing houses. Most of these were old, and few had proper plumbing. Yet local health inspectors usually turned a blind eye to the filth and the over-crowding. If they had applied the law strictly, many families would have lost their homes.

The new London County Council slowly came to see how the problem could be solved. It started its housing programme in a small way. First it finished slum clearance plans which meant building flats to provide for families whose homes were pulled down. The first two blocks are still lived in: at Boundary Street, Shoreditch (1895) and Millbank (1899). This did not, however, add to London's total stock of housing. The LCC realized that private builders could never provide enough homes for Londoners with low incomes. The Council must build and rent out homes itself, and on a large scale.

Though land in central London was very dear, there were plenty of cheap sites further out. If only cheap transport could be laid on, poorer people too could live in the suburbs. The LCC first bought land in Tooting, Tottenham and Hammersmith. Here they built 'cottage estates', each family having its own house and garden. The rents were lower than for privately built houses. The rooms were smaller, but the houses were solidly made. Many of the cottages were pleasant to look at; some were laid out in quiet closes among trees. 1299 houses and four shops were built on the Totterdown estate at Tooting.

Flats at Millbank built by the LCC in 1899.

The first cottage estate, built by the LCC at Totterdown Fields in 1903.

Nearly half the new tenants worked in central London. They travelled by the electric tramcars opened by the LCC the year before.

By 1914, 10 000 people lived in LCC—owned homes. Similar flats and cottages were also built by councils in the outer boroughs. After the war, with money provided by the government, the LCC and other councils decided to build on a much bigger scale. They still kept to the same general pattern. This meant flats in the centre (often replacing further slums which were pulled down) and cottage estates in the suburbs. Blocks of flats were never more than five floors high, because lifts were thought to be too expensive. Most of these blocks were built in a rather formal style based on Georgian houses.

The houses on the cottage estates were more comfortable than the pre-1914 models. The rooms were larger and they now all had baths. Then the 1929–31 slump cut the amount that could be spent on each house. Some of the 1930s estates are more skimpily built than the 1920s ones.

Transport

London's transport system spread outwards with the new houses (and sometimes even got there first). Horse trams had been running almost as long as horse buses. The first electric tram was opened from Shepherd's Bush to Acton, in one direction and to Kew Bridge in the other. The power was taken from overhead cables. These privately-owned tramways quickly spread a network of lines over the north and west suburbs. Meanwhile the LCC had also started tram routes,

The Tram terminus at Shepherds Bush. The photograph was taken on August Bank holiday, yet people are wearing thick clothes and hats.

mainly in east and central London (including the one to the cottage estate at Tooting).

Gradually the two systems came to work together. By 1914 there were LCC-owned tramlines in central London linking with privately owned lines in the suburbs. This meant you could travel by tram from Barnet in Hertfordshire to Purley in Surrey. The tramlines opened up new housing sites, just as the railways had done in Victorian times.

London's first motor buses appeared in 1899. Nobody liked them at first; they were noisy and smelly and often broke down. That changed in 1910 when the London General Omnibus Company brought in its 'B type' bus. This was quiet and reliable, and cheap to run. The public flocked to ride on them and many new bus routes were opened. There was soon no place in all London that was not within walking distance of a bus or tram stop.

In the end the buses put the trams out of business. They could adapt better to heavy traffic, and they needed no lines or cables. For a while it looked as if they might even kill the new tube trains as well.

The first electric underground line, from King William Street (in the City) to Stockwell, had opened in 1890. Next, the big Metropolitan and District Underground Railway Companies began trying out electric trains in place of their steam engines. Then a completely new company, the Central London Railway, opened the first tube line in 1900. It ran from the Bank to Shepherd's Bush. Soon 100 000 people a day were using it, all for a flat fare of twopence.

Several other tube lines were planned. But they did not make much progress until an energetic American, Charles Yerckes, took over. In 1901 he bought the District Line and also built an electric power station at Lots Road in Chelsea. Then he bought several other companies with plans to build tubes. Electricity from Lots Road could provide power for them all.

Yerckes' new tube lines ran at right angles to the Central Line. The Baker Street–Waterloo line was ready by 1906. At once a newspaper gave

Hampstead Garden Suburb being built, 1911–12. A view down Erskine Hill towards the fields of Finchley. The Suburb was within easy walking distance of Golders Green Station.

it the nick-name Bakerloo. The Piccadilly line, from Finsbury Park to Hammersmith, opened later the same year. In 1907 came the Hampstead line (now part of the Northern), from the Strand to Golders Green.

Sometimes it was almost a matter of chance where one of these new lines ended. In 1902 Charles Yerckes and a friend drove out north in a hansom cab looking for a good place for the final station of their new Hampstead tube. They stopped first at Hampstead Heath, but decided against a site here. Instead they went on through open fields to the cross-roads at Golders Green. Yerckes saw that this was a place where a new railway would attract house builders. For a short while the new station was the only building in the area, but within a few months estate agents were busy and soon houses were being built all round.

All these different tubes ran as completely separate lines for several years. They were only linked up when Charing Cross Underground station was rebuilt as a junction in 1914 (it is now called Embankment).

After the First World War tubes and underground lines were built even further into the outer suburbs. First, part of the Northern Line was run on out to Edgware in 1924. At the same time a big advertising campaign invited people to come and live nearby. One clever estate agent opened an office in Edgware a few weeks before the new railway was finished. The railway company hired a marquee and gave a party for the official opening. Leading local people were invited and offered free cigars and champagne. Then the manager of the line proudly told the Press his plans. Trains would run every eight minutes in the rush hour, every ten at other times. You would reach Charing Cross from Edgware in thirty-five minutes.

The Bakerloo was built out to Stanmore in 1932. A few months later the Piccadilly line was opened to Cockfosters. Southwards, a new line stretched to Morden; eastwards, to Upminster. The other Northern line grew later. In fact the Second World War had started before the High Barnet and Mill Hill lines were opened (in 1940–1). All this time the Southern Railway was converting its lines through south London (and beyond) to electricity.

In their early years all these different kinds of transport were rivals. Tubes, underground, trams and buses were competing with each other for customers. This should have brought good service and cheap fares. Instead, it often meant muddle and waste. Finally, the government stepped in and persuaded them to work together. The result was the London Passenger Transport Board, created by Act of Parliament in 1933.

The government did not only help with advice. It lent money for the big railway building projects. It also paid for many miles of new main roads. These were to provide for all the new cars and lorries pouring onto the roadways in the 1930s. Morris and Ford's new cheap models made it possible for many Londoners to own cars for the first time. Now they could drive out to the country along several fast new roads: Eastern and Western Avenues, the Great Cambridge Road, the Kingston By-pass. There was also the North Circular Road, running in a huge semi-circle through the north London suburbs.

Soon houses and factories were lining the new roads. This was called 'ribbon development'. But these buildings spoilt the whole point of the new roads for they clogged them up with local traffic when they were supposed to be fast

Ribbon development along the Great West Road.

throughways. Parliament passed an act to stop ribbon development in 1935, but it was too late to undo the damage.

Shopping and Entertainment

Gordon Selfridge had made a great success of his shops in America. In 1909 he opened a huge department store in Oxford Street. He brought his own American architect and window dresser, and they helped to make this the most modern shop in London. Other shop-owners followed Selfridge's example. By the 1930s Oxford Street had more big shops than any other road in London. Among them were Marks and Spencer and Woolworth. Woolworth was American-owned, but Marks and Spencer had started in Leeds. By 1914 it had thirty branches in London.

Another new building appeared in many local shopping centres: a cinema. The earliest one still in use is the tiny Bioscope near Victoria Station. Some cinemas were converted theatres, such as the Empire, Leicester Square. Golders Green had the first talkie cinema, the Lido, opened in 1928. These later cinemas were much bigger than the early ones. By the 1930s most people were going to the cinema at least once a week. So the new cinemas held audiences of 1000 and more. Their names made you think of riches and glamour—Ritz, Plaza, Regal, Majestic.

The Regal Cinema, Uxbridge. Today many of these huge cinemas have been divided into three smaller ones, or turned into bingo halls.

Down by the Thames in Savoy Hill the BBC sent out its first broadcasts in 1922. It grew so quickly that soon a much larger building was needed. Broadcasting House, opened in 1931, was designed to fit at the curving lower end of Portland Place. Overseas broadcasts needed further space still so Bush House was built to house them at the foot of Kingsway.

Business and Industry

Many of the new buildings in central London in the 1920s and 30s were blocks of offices. There were big new government offices, there were headquarters buildings for new groups of companies. New bodies like the London Passenger Transport Board needed a large central office block. When the London docks came under one management, the Port of London Authority, that needed a new building too. So did the LCC, which began its new offices at County Hall in 1912.

A company might open a grand office in the City while its factories were many miles away.

The Senate House, London University.

Land in central London was much too expensive to be used for factory sites. From 1900 onwards more and more firms moved outwards when they wanted to expand. Industry needs good transport as well as cheap land. So the new factories were mostly in the Lea Valley and parts of the north and west suburbs. Here there were canals, railways, and main roads. Many products in daily use were made in factories on the western edge of London. Good fast roads could take them easily into the West End shops and showrooms.

Furniture and clothing firms had often made several moves before they ended up in the Lea Valley, for example. From the City they had moved to Shoreditch, then to Bethnal Green, before going further out still. Here they joined new industries like radio and electric appliances.

London was luckier than northern England during the Slump. Her industries—light engineering, food, chemicals, clothing, printing—all kept going reasonably well.

The Two World Wars

The First World War did not change the look of London. There was little bombing (though a German airship crashed north of the suburbs at Potters Bar). Afterwards the Cenotaph was built in the widest part of Whitehall as a memorial to those who had lost their lives. Here the Queen and Prime Minister go each November to lay a wreath of poppies.

The Second World War, on the other hand, made huge changes because so much was destroyed by bombing. The government knew in advance that heavy air raids were likely. They started to make plans when they saw that war was coming near. Women and children were to be evacuated from London and other big cities. Rest centres were prepared, and air raid wardens were trained.

Evacuation actually began on 1 September 1939 (two days before the official outbreak of war). One and a half million people left London for safe places in the country. Among them there were 800 000 children without their parents.

It was the end of a long, hot summer. Some

Evacuees leaving a London station, September 1939.

people were only just back from the seaside. Many families had not yet bought winter clothes. The children were told to report to their schools with one small suitcase. They also needed a label round their neck with their name written on it. Each school marched its pupils to the nearest railway station, and put them on the first empty train.

For days parents did not know where their children had been taken. Most London boys and girls found themselves in homes very different from their own. They struck the country people as being dirty, rude and raggedly dressed. Mothers and babies from London slums also got a cool welcome. A great many people decided to come back to London and risk the bombs. Those who stayed on found that the villagers grew more friendly as they got used to each other.

Almost a whole year passed and no bombs fell on London. Country after country in Europe fell to Hitler's armies. The Battle of Britain was fought over south-east England. But still the expected bomb attack did not come.

Then on 24 August 1940 some German pilots who thought they were over the sea let a few surplus bombs drop on London. The next night British planes bombed Berlin in revenge. The real bombing of London began on 6 September and went on without stopping until May 1941. Hitler hoped he would break London's spirit by this huge attack. He had failed to invade England; instead, he hoped to persuade her to surrender by destroying her capital.

The first big raids were on the East End of London. People who lost their homes were given a bed in a rest centre. One centre, in West Ham, had a direct hit, killing 450 people. The attacks moved to the West End later in the month. Several bombs fell on Buckingham Palace on 15 September.

People tried to carry on their normal lives by day. But at night, when the bombers came, many went to air-raid shelters. The official public shelters were not at all popular. Most of them were just concrete boxes, and often dark and damp. Families often preferred their own shelter at home. This could be an Anderson shelter made of corrugated iron, or a Morrison shelter inside a house.

Many people felt still safer sheltering far underground in a tube station. The government did not encourage them; but it could not stop them buying train tickets and staying the night. Some families sent a child on ahead each afternoon to take over a piece of platform. By evening every space was filled with mattresses and blankets. Only a narrow strip at the front of the platform stayed empty, as the trains went on running till 10.30 each night. No one got much sleep till after that.

London was carefully organized into districts

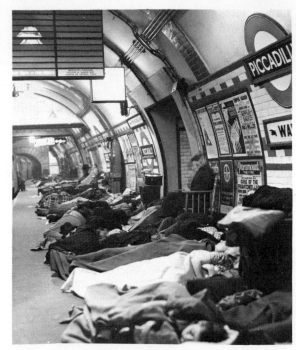

Night scene on a tube station platform.

A family going into its Anderson shelter.

for coping with air-raid damage. The headquarters was in the Geology Museum at South Kensington. Every group of streets had its local Air Raid Warden's Post. There were roughly ten for each square mile. The strongest building in the area was chosen for it. Sandbags were piled against the walls to make it safer still. Inside there was a table, camp beds, telephone, maps and a tea-pot and kettle. Every bomb that fell would first be reported here. The warden then alerted the fire brigade, ambulance or heavy rescue brigade if they were needed.

The weeks of bombing lengthened into months. Each raid left more Londoners without homes. In Stepney four houses in every ten were damaged or destroyed. Over London as a whole, one person in six was made homeless or 'bombed out'. Many streets were blocked with rubble. At Balham there was a bomb crater so large that a bus fell right into it.

The worst raids were on moonlit nights. There was a very heavy attack on the City on 29 December 1940. Fire bombs (incendiaries) set one building alight after another. The flames leapt across gaps until a huge area was alight. It

St Paul's Cathedral among the ruins. An unexploded bomb fell close to the cathedral on 12 September 1940, and began to slip down towards the foundations. Three days later it was dug out by bomb disposal experts and driven at top speed to Hackney Marshes, where it exploded.

stretched west of Moorgate right across the area where London's Roman fort had once stood.

Another specially bad raid was on 10 May 1941, a night of full moon. Many famous buildings were hit, including Westminster Abbey, the Law Courts and the Tower. A gin depot in the City Road blazed fiercely. So did books at the British Museum. But the fires were controlled here, and the buildings were not all destroyed. Next morning clouds of brown smoke blotted out the sun. Some of the fires went on burning for eleven days. Many main streets were blocked with fallen buildings. Most of the railway stations were out of action for a while. But worst of all, 1436 people had been killed that night. About one million houses were destroyed or damaged in the London Blitz.

The heavy raid in May was also one of the last—for the time being. Hitler switched his bombers to attack Russia in the summer of 1941. There were more big raids in the spring of 1943, and again in early 1944. In the summer of 1944 the first of the V1s arrived. These were self-propelled bombs which made a whirring noise as they passed overhead. If you heard the noise stop, you knew the 'doodlebug' was about to plunge down to earth.

That September an even more sinister weapon started to arrive: the V2 rockets. These came too swiftly to give any warning, and they did much more damage than the V1s. They went on coming until late March 1945.

London was a badly battered city by the time Germany was beaten (in May 1945). Yet the courage of the Londoners had stayed high all through the bombing. Hitler made a grave mistake in thinking he could crush their spirit.

A great many famous buildings were damaged or destroyed. So was a large amount of slum property, and huge numbers of good houses and flats. Everyone was determined to make the new London a better place to live in than the old.

London since 1945

London has not grown outwards since the war. But her buildings have grown taller, and in the outer areas they are thicker on the ground. Many places once had big Victorian villas set in gardens. Now they have blocks of flats, or rows of three-storey terrace houses.

In the City, the skyline has changed completely. Looking down from a high place like Hampstead Heath, St Paul's used to be the tallest building. Now it is far out-topped by lofty office blocks. Among them stand the elegant towers of the Barbican scheme. Here the City Council is bringing people back to live in the very heart of London.

These tall offices have been built in the sixties and seventies. Straight after the war the first priority was to build new homes. London had over 100 000 homes completely destroyed by bombs, and another million damaged.

The LCC and other local councils in outer London did the great bulk of the re-building.

Part of the Barbican development in the City, with the church of St Giles, Cripplegate, on the left.

They set a target of 100 000 new homes. At first the planners carried on with the pre-war pattern of flats in the centre and houses in the suburbs. Then experts saw the benefits of mixing types of homes. A better blend of age and income groups was achieved in this way. The first mixed estate was the Ackroyden at Wimbledon, opened in 1953. A much bigger experiment followed at Roehampton. Here 11-floor blocks of flats were placed among 4-floor maisonettes and 2-floor cottages.

Land was scarce and expensive. The LCC decided to send some of the people waiting for homes to new towns right outside London (Crawley, Hemel Hempstead and Harlow were some of these). Another solution was to build even bigger blocks of flats. The taller the block, the more space is left free round its base. 'Point' and 'Slab' blocks rose higher and higher. For example, the Pepys Estate at Greenwich had three 24-storey blocks; but by the time it was built in 1966, people were turning against high-rise flats. Mothers with young children felt terribly lonely in them. They might be shut in all day, far above ground level. Everyone suffered when the lifts broke down. So the GLC (the LCC became the Greater London Council in

High Rise flats: Alton West Estate at Roehampton, opened in 1959.

1965) has gone back to lower buildings. There are more maisonettes and cottages, and blocks of flats are lower now.

Private housing got going more slowly after the war. There have been blocks of luxury flats in central London, and a great many terraces of town houses in the suburbs. Large new houses are rare, because site and building costs are so high now.

All over London there are new schools, libraries, swimming pools, hospitals and so on. Yet a great many old buildings are still in use. There is not enough money to replace all the Victorian schools, or all the old hospitals which were once workhouses. However much the GLC builds, it never keeps pace with demand. This is partly because people's standards have risen. Every family wants a self-contained home with proper heating and plumbing. As well as this, more people have come to live in London from overseas. But fewer people live in the centre now. It is in the outer boroughs that the population is still rising.

Transport has changed since 1945. Far more Londoners now own cars; many travel to work in them. Flyovers, underpasses and roundabouts have been built to cope with the increase. But most Londoners still travel to work by tube, underground and bus. As the number of offices has increased, so have the crowds at the stations and bus stops in the rush hours. London Transport wants to build new tube lines to relieve the pressure. But these are now very costly. The new Victoria Line was held up for seven years till the government at last provided the money (it opened in 1968–9). The latest tube line, the Jubilee, is still under construction.

The greatest growth of all has been in air traffic. Croydon Aerodrome served London before the war. Afterwards, Northolt was used for a few years. Meanwhile a huge new airport was being built at Heathrow, on the western edge of London. This is now the busiest airport in the world, and it is still growing.

Houses, roads and schools have been the first need since the war. But London has also gained some fine public buildings. The Royal Festival Hall (opened in the year of the Festival of Britain, 1951) is admired all over the world.

The South Bank, showing Waterloo Bridge and the Festival Hall. With three concert halls, an art gallery, a cinema and the National Theatre, the South Bank has become a great entertainments centre.

Recently (1977) the National Theatre was opened as the latest addition to the South Bank Arts complex.

In 2000 years London has grown from nothing to a great city in which more than eight million people live. During this time there have been many changes, only some of which are mentioned in this book. But through nearly every period, one thing has remained true: people are proud to be Londoners and like living in London. Today, foreigners who have visited many other capital cities say that London is the pleasantest to live in. Long may it remain so!

Questions on Twentieth Century London

1 Imagine a family in 1927 going to look at two new houses in the suburbs, and deciding to buy one of them. What might influence their choice?

2 Try to find out what bomb damage was done in your district of London. Older neighbours will be able to help you.

3 Describe how the LCC and GLC took an increasing share in providing homes for Londoners, 1900–1970.

4 How can you travel to (a) the City, (b) the West End from your home, using train, car, underground or bus?

5 Do you like living in London? Try to think why you do (or why you don't).

6 Make a list of ways in which you think London could be made a better place to live in.

Where to Go and What to See

The best place to start is the Museum of London. This is in the City, close to the Barbican Underground Station. It shows the whole history of London from prehistoric times to the present day. Here you will find objects dug up or found or made in London, all set out in display cases which explain their background. There are also whole rooms to help you imagine life in London in the past: for example, life-size models of a Roman living-room and kitchen, and actual shop-fronts and panelled rooms from buildings which were pulled down.

This is much the richest collection showing London's history. In the following sections other museums are mentioned which display some special topic.

After your visits to Museums, try to get out into the streets of London to see the famous buildings you have read about. Everywhere mentioned in these sections is open to the public. Normally, visiting hours are 10 am to 5 pm on weekdays, 2–5 pm on Sundays; but it would be wise to check, as more places are now closing on Mondays.

Roman London

The British Museum has a gallery on Roman Britain, containing many objects found in London. Look for Julianus Classicianus' tomb, and the mosaic of Bacchus on a tiger.

The kiln from Highgate Wood is in the Horniman Museum, Forest Hill. You can see the Roman wall in several places. There are two very good pieces near Tower Hill Underground station; in Wakefield Gardens, and Cooper's Row (behind an office block called Midland House). Another good stretch is in St Alphage's churchyard by the modern street called London Wall. In all three, the Roman parts are at the bottom, with medieval additions above them.

The foundations of a turret from the Fort can be seen from the pavement in Noble Street, just south of the Museum of London.

The Temple of Mithras is in front of Bucklersbury House in Queen Victoria Street (all the treasures dug up here are in the Museum of London).

Medieval London

The Tower of London is the biggest medieval building in the City. The White Tower is the original Norman keep, and should be visited first. Most of the rooms are used to display armour and weapons, but the Chapel of St John has not been altered.

Two medieval parish churches that are specially worth visiting both started as chapels for monks or nuns. St Bartholomew-the-Great in Smithfield was part of a priory; St Helen's, just off Bishopsgate, has a double nave (originally one half was for the people of the parish, the other half for the nuns).

All Hallows Barking (near the Tower) and St Giles, Cripplegate (in the Barbican), have always been parish churches.

The Temple Church (just south of Fleet Street) and St John's, Clerkenwell, were both part of the headquarters of Orders of Knights.

The Charterhouse (in Charterhouse Square), once a Carthusian Monastery, is only open on Wednesday afternoons in summer.

The Guildhall's Great Hall and Crypt are open, but both have been much altered and mended since medieval times.

Crosby Hall can be seen on Chelsea Embankment, where it was moved from Bishopsgate. It is the dining-room of a Students' hostel now.

London's two greatest medieval churches are outside the City: Westminster Abbey (go out of the north door into the cloister, and see the Chapter House and Crypt Museum); and Southwark Cathedral (originally the Abbey of St Mary Overy).

The street along the river behind the Cathedral leads to the remains of the Bishop of Winchester's Palace, and the site of the Globe Theatre.

Don't forget Westminster Hall, built by William

Rufus, which is easiest to visit on a tour of the Houses of Parliament.

Tudor London

The Victoria and Albert Museum contains the front of Sir Paul Pinder's house from Bishopsgate, complete panelled rooms and the Great Bed of Ware.

Staple Inn in High Holborn is the only black-and-white timber building left (apart from the Queen's House in the Tower). Notice the overhanging storeys and the steep gables. It was built to provide rooms for lawyers, and is now used as offices.

Middle Temple Hall is difficult to visit, because it is still used for lawyers' dinners, but it is officially open daily for short times.

All the Inns of Court are open to the public to walk through. Lincoln's Inn also has Tudor buildings.

St James's Palace is not open to the public, but you can see it from Marlborough Gate or St James's Street.

Stuart London

The Geffrye Museum in Kingsland Road, Shoreditch, uses a building which started off as an almshouse (built by a Lord Mayor of London in 1715). Each room is furnished in the style of a different period, and it is specially well equipped for school parties.

The Banqueting House in Whitehall, the Queen's House, Greenwich, and the Church of St Paul's, Covent Garden were all designed by Inigo Jones.

Kensington Palace has very fine State Apartments. William III bought the original house and had it turned into a palace by Sir Christopher Wren.

St Paul's Cathedral and the many parish churches rebuilt after the Great Fire were all designed by Wren. St Mary-le-Bow is a good one to choose.

The Monument, in Fish Street, commemorates the Fire. St Olave's, Hart Street, was Samuel Pepys' parish church. It contains monuments to both Pepys and his wife. Houses of the type built after the fire can be seen in Queen Anne's Gate, and Broadwick Street, Soho.

Georgian London

Sir John Soane's Museum, Lincoln's Inn Fields, is the house of an eighteenth-century art lover. Both the house and its contents are interesting. This is also true of Dr Johnson's House in Gough Square, off Fleet Street.

Boodles' Club is in St James's Street (designed by J. Crunden in the same style as the Adams Brothers used). There are two shops opposite which still use their eighteenth-century premises—Lock's the Hatters, and Berry Bros, wine merchants.

Somerset House is sometimes open for exhibitions, and you can always walk into the courtyard, off the Strand.

St Martin in the Fields and St George's, Hanover Square, are in the West End, but there are also very fine churches of this period in Limehouse and Spitalfields.

You can walk round the squares of Mayfair; St James's, Grosvenor, Hanover, Cavendish and Berkeley Squares, but you will find very few of the original houses. Clive's House in Berkeley Square is one of them.

Bedford, Russell and Tavistock Squares, built later, contain far more of the original houses.

There are also many Georgian houses in other parts of central London, in Kennington Park Road and Canonbury Square, for example.

Regency London

The British Museum and the National Gallery were both given new buildings in this period.

Apsley House (at Hyde Park Corner) was once the Duke of Wellington's home, and is now the Wellington Museum.

You can follow Nash's route for the Prince Regent all the way from Carlton House Terrace (by the Mall) to Regent's Park, going up Regent Street and crossing Piccadilly and Oxford Circuses on the way. Nearly all his big terraces in Regent's Park are still standing; Cumberland and Hanover are very fine.

Several of the big clubs in Pall Mall are still in their original buildings, the Athenaeum and Reform Clubs for example.

Victorian London

The Victoria and Albert Museum and the Natural History Museum are both in South Kensington. The V and A has a room designed by William Morris as well as many objects from this and earlier times.

The Houses of Parliament (easiest to visit when Parliament is not sitting).

The Law Courts in the Strand.

St Pancras and Paddington Stations.

Private houses at Princes Gate and Lancaster Gate (on each side of Hyde Park).

There are many Victorian Gothic houses and churches in the London suburbs.

The Crystal Palace was burnt down, but Alexandra Palace is still standing, north-west of Muswell Hill.

The Operating Theatre of old St Thomas's Hospital shows you what it was like to be ill in the early part of the nineteenth century. You can get in through St Thomas's Church, St Thomas Street, Southwark. The hospital moved in 1865 to Lambeth, opposite the Houses of Parliament. It is being re-built, but some of the original wards (designed with advice from Florence Nightingale) are still in use.

Acknowledgments

The Publishers would like to thank the following who have provided illustrations:
Aerofilms Limited: 22, 99; B. T. Batsford (Photograph: National Monuments Record): 90; Debbie Beevor: 5, 8, 15; British Library: 34(b), 40; British Museum: 9(b), 10, 12(b); 14(t), 17, 65 (t); *Country Life:* 31(b); Devonshire Collection Chatsworth. Reproduced by permission of The Trustees: 50(b); Richard Einsig: 104(t), 105; A. B. Gillmore and the Greater London Council: 104(b); Greater London Council (courtesy Peter Jackson): 94; The Greater London Council Photograph Library: 43(t), 61, 86(t), 91, 92(b), 96, 97(t), 100(t), 100(r); The Greater London Council Print Collection: 63(t), 63(b), 64(l), 69(t), 82; Grosvenor Museum, Chester: 11(t); Hampstead Garden Suburb Archive: 98; The Illustrated London News: 79(b), 84; Peter Jackson Collection: 24(t), 53(r), 58, 72, 93; A. F. Kersting: 31(t), 32, 33, 35, 42, 66(b); Courtesy of the London Borough of Harrow (Library Services): 95; The London Society: 81; London Transport Executive: 97(b); Mansell Collection: 12(t), 19(b), 44, 50(t), 51(t), 53(l), 77; The Museum of London: 9(t), 11(b), 13, 14(c), 14(b), 16, 26, 27, 29, 37, 38, 39, 41, 43, 48, 49(t), 49(b), 51(b), 52, 55, 56, 59, 60, 62, 64(r), 67, 69(b), 73, 74, 75, 78, 79(t), 83, 85, 89; Courtesy of Professor A. R. Myers: 20; The National Gallery, London. Reproduced by courtesy of the Trustees: 66; National Monuments Record: 28, 34(t), 47, 92(t); Radio Times Hulton Picture Library: 19(t), 24(b), 25, 46(b), 86(b), 101, 102(t), 102(b), 103; Victoria and Albert Museum: 87, 88; Wayland Picture Library: 46(t); Weaver-Smith Collection: 54; Courtesy of the Trustees of the Wellcome Institute (photograph Peter Jackson): 70.

Index of People

(Numbers in italics are references which occur in captions to pictures)

Index of Places

(Numbers in italics are references which occur in captions to pictures)